HARCOURT

# Math

## Practice Workbook

Grade 4

Orlando • Boston • Dallas • Chicago • San Diego
www.harcourtschool.com

Printed in the United States of America

ISBN 0-15-320769-8

15 16 073 10 09 08 07

# CONTENTS

## Unit 8: MEASUREMENT AND GEOMETRY

### Chapter 23: Customary Measurement



### Chapter 24: Metric Measurement



### Chapter 25: Perimeter and Area of Plane Figures



### Chapter 26: Solid Figures and Volume



## Unit 9: PROBABILITY, ALGEBRA, AND GRAPHING

### Chapter 27: Outcomes



### Chapter 28: Probability



### Chapter 29: Algebra: Explore Negative Numbers



### Chapter 30: Explore the Coordinate Grid

Name ______________________________



# Benchmark Numbers

## Vocabulary

Fill in the blank.

**1.** A ______________ is a known number of things that helps you understand the size or amount of a different number of things.

Use the benchmark to decide which is the more reasonable number.

**2.** Pennies in the jar

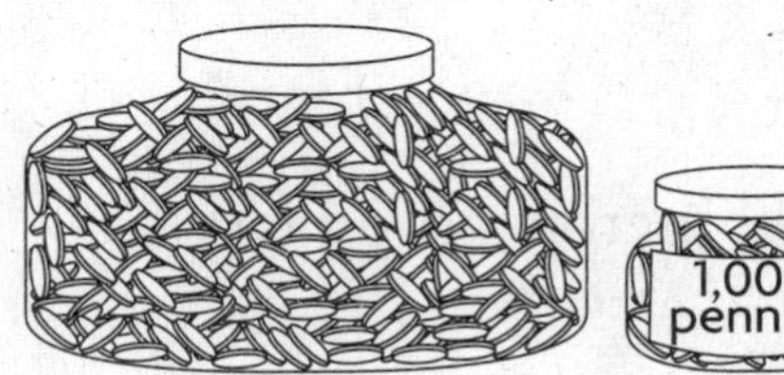


500 or 5,000

______________

**3.** Houses in the neighborhood

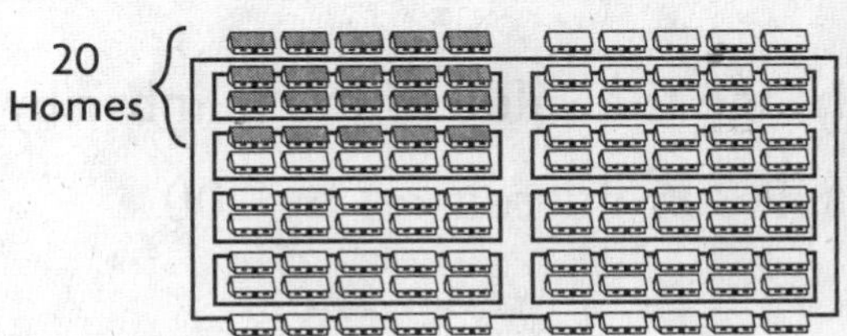


100 or 1,000

______________

**4.** Height of a shrub

20 inches or 200 inches

______________

**5.** Books on a shelf

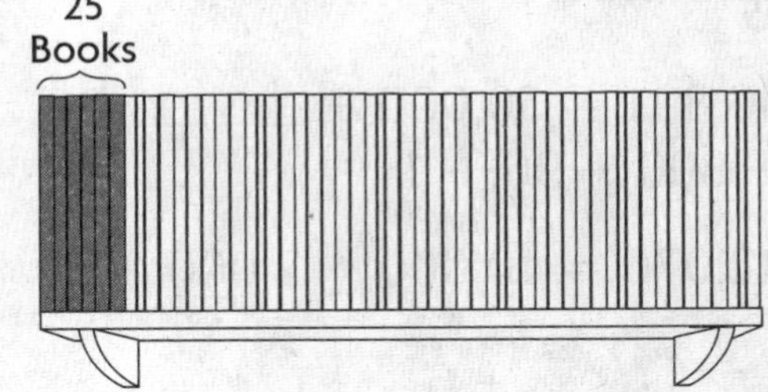


200 or 2,000

______________

## Mixed Review

**6.** $3 + 8$

**7.** $9 + 5$

**8.** $16 + 12$

**9.** $24 + 51$

**10.** $45 + 22$

**11.** $31 + 18$

**12.** $44 + 29$

**13.** $35 - 17$

**14.** $35 - 27$

**15.** $59 - 31$

**16.** 12 +11 ________

**17.** 19 + 49 ________

**18.** 62 + 21 ________

Name ____________________



# Understand Place Value

Write the value of the digit 3 in each number.

1. 4,389 ________
2. 3,270 ________
3. 56,223 ________
4. 78,530 ________

Compare the digits to find the value of the change.

5. 67,335 to 47,335 ________
6. 45,289 to 45,889 ________
7. 48,367 to 42,367 ________

Change the value of the number by the given amount.

8. 2,305 decreased by 200 ________
9. 72,358 increased by 6,000 ________
10. 46,883 decreased by 40 ________
11. 29,402 increased by 40,000 ________

Complete.

12. 56,891 = 50,000 + ________ + 800 + 90 + 1
13. ________6,408 = 80,000 + 6,000 + 400 + 8
14. 42,076 = 40,000 + 2,000 + ________ + 6
15. 37,905 = ________ + 7,000 + 900 + 5

## Mixed Review

16. 420 + 307 + 21
17. 818 + 128 + 66
18. 77 + 20 + 18
19. 213 + 501 + 190
20. 633 + 409 + 7
21. 100 − 22
22. 87 − 24
23. 98 − 69
24. 53 − 8
25. 110 − 56

Name ______________________________

# Problem Solving Skill

## Use a Graph

The United States Department of Agriculture has named 5 food groups and recommends a maximum number of daily servings from each group.

| Maximum Daily Servings | |
|---|---|
| dairy | ◎ ◖ |
| meat | ◎ ◖ |
| vegetables | ◎ ◎ ◖ |
| fruit | ◎ ◎ |
| bread and cereal | ◎ ◎ ◎ ◎ ◎ ◖ |

Key: Each ◎ stands for 2 servings.

For 1–8, use the graph.

**1.** What is the maximum recommended number of meat servings?

______________________________

**2.** Which two food groups have the same number of recommended servings?

______________________________

**3.** Of which food groups can you eat more than four servings per day?

______________________________

**4.** Of which food group can you eat the most servings?

______________________________

**5.** Today, Erika ate 5 servings of meat. How would you represent this on the pictograph?

______________________________

**6.** What is the total number of fruit and vegetable servings recommended?

______________________________

**7.** Rolanda has eaten 7 servings from the bread and cereal group today. How many more servings should she have?

______________________________

**8.** At breakfast, Jamika's banana counted as 2 fruit servings. How many more fruit servings should she have today?

______________________________

## Mixed Review

What is the value of the digit 7?

**9.** 1,762 ______________

**10.** 7,900,631 ______________

**11.** 44,072,461 ______________

**12.** 817,535 ______________

Name ____________________



# Compare Numbers

Write the greater number.

1. 3,568 or 3,658 ______
2. 8,468 or 8,482 ______
3. 35,689 or 34,690 ______
4. 8,948 or 21,385 ______
5. 389,584 or 388,499 ______
6. 3,843,982 or 3,847,302 ______
7. 25,679 or 22,329 ______
8. 3,457,822 or 3,458,835 ______
9. 9,248,355 or 924,835 ______

Compare. Write <, >, or = in each ○.

10. 3,489 ○ 3,578
11. 25,899 ○ 25,890
12. 75,673 ○ 75,673
13. 3,142,355 ○ 314,235
14. 33,452,236 ○ 35,235,032

Find all of the digits that can replace each □.

15. 6□7,348 < 647,348 ______
16. 35,468,245 < 35,468,□45 ______

## Mixed Review

17. Write 8,000,000 + 30,000 + 5,000 + 400 + 30 + 2 in standard form. ______
18. Write 32,883 in word form. ______
19. What digit is in the ten thousands place in 32,456,922? ______
20. Write the value of the digit 8 in the number 385,722. ______
21. Round 7,899 to the nearest hundred. ______
22. Round 42,616 to the nearest ten. ______

Name ______________________________



## Order Numbers

Write the numbers in order from *least* to *greatest*.

**1.** 15,867; 15,394; 15,948; 15,493

______________________

**2.** 65,447; 65,743; 65,446, 65,395

______________________

**3.** 249,330; 247,449; 248,390

______________________

**4.** 3,456,490; 3,458,395; 3,359,498

______________________

Write the numbers in order from *greatest* to *least*.

**5.** 45,387; 48,339; 47,110

______________________

**6.** 252,484; 259,793; 258,932

______________________

**7.** 2,783,859; 2,788,394; 2,937,383

______________________

**8.** 360,839; 45,395; 366,395

______________________

**9.** 4,671,302; 4,716,230; 4,716,200

______________________

**10.** 740,516; 74,506; 740,605

______________________

Name all of the digits that can replace each □.

**11.** $4,599 < 4,63\square < 4,634$

______________________

**12.** $3,554,684 > 3,\square 69,304 > 3,184,394$

______________________

### Mixed Review

**13.** $\begin{array}{r} 25 \\ +\ 42 \\ \hline \end{array}$

**14.** $\begin{array}{r} 99 \\ 21 \\ +\ 86 \\ \hline \end{array}$

**15.** $\begin{array}{r} 95¢ \\ -\ 43¢ \\ \hline \end{array}$

**16.** $\begin{array}{r} 78¢ \\ -\ 24¢ \\ \hline \end{array}$

**17.** $\begin{array}{r} 13 \\ 74 \\ +\ 26 \\ \hline \end{array}$

**18.** Stacey jogged for 25 minutes on Saturday and 38 minutes on Tuesday. How much longer did she jog on Tuesday than on Saturday?

______________________

**19.** Rolanda completed 12 homework problems before dinner and 18 after dinner. How many homework problems did she complete altogether?

______________________

Name ______________________



# Problem Solving Strategy

## Make a Table

Make a table to solve.

| Desert | Continent | Area (sq mi) |
|---|---|---|
| | | |
| | | |
| | | |
| | | |

The Sahara Desert in Africa has an area of 3,500,000 square miles. The Simpson Desert in Australia has an area of 56,000 square miles. In North America, the Mojave Desert has an area of 15,000 square miles; and the Kalahari Desert in Africa has an area of 275,000 square miles.

1. Which desert has the greatest area?

   ______________________

2. Which two deserts are located on the same continent?

   ______________________

3. Which deserts have an area of less than 100,000 square miles?

   ______________________

4. On which continent is the desert with the least area located?

   ______________________

## Mixed Review

5. Write 3,000,000 + 20,000 + 5,000 + 300 + 70 + 2 in standard form.

   ______________________

6. Write the numbers in order from *least* to *greatest*: 254,879; 2,254,920; 1,678,305; 353,502.

   ______________________

   ______________________

Compare. Write <, >, or = in the ◯.

7. 354,992 ◯ 288,492

8. 7,394,398 ◯ 7,394,398

9. 394,234 ◯ 3,294,394

10. 6,187,249 ◯ 61,872,490

11. $\begin{array}{r} 9{,}421{,}720 \\ -\ 6{,}198{,}135 \\ \hline \end{array}$

12. $\begin{array}{r} 210{,}076 \\ +\ 935{,}811 \\ \hline \end{array}$

13. $\begin{array}{r} 8{,}176{,}553 \\ +\ \ \ 30{,}602 \\ \hline \end{array}$

14. $\begin{array}{r} 172{,}442 \\ -\ 172{,}435 \\ \hline \end{array}$

15. 786 − 421 = ________

16. 2,779 − 460 = ________

Name ______________________________



# Round Numbers

Round each number to the nearest thousand.

1. 5,339 ________
2. 9,895 ________
3. 75,367 ________
4. 22,022 ________
5. 5,600,679 ________
6. 1,354,029 ________
7. 283,966 ________
8. 636,592 ________

Round each number to the place of the underlined digit.

9. $\underline{6}$,333 ________
10. 8$\underline{3}$7 ________
11. 8,$\underline{0}$21 ________
12. 4$\underline{5}$,935 ________
13. 356,8$\underline{8}$2 ________
14. 5$\underline{0}$2,446 ________
15. 24,$\underline{5}$46 ________
16. 8$\underline{8}$8,044 ________
17. $\underline{4}$7,164 ________
18. $\underline{1}$,999,444 ________
19. $\underline{1}$,366,901 ________
20. 9,$\underline{2}$03,774 ________

## Mixed Review

21. $9 + 4 + 5 =$ ____
22. $27 + 33 + 59 =$ ____
23. $48 - 29 =$ ____

24. $6 \times 2$

25. $8 \times 5$

26. $9 \times 8$

27. $7 \times 7$

28. What is the value of the digit 7 in 478,394?

________

29. What is the value of the digit 5 in 5,394,332?

________

# Estimate Sums and Differences

Estimate the sum or difference.

1. 7,379 + 5,496

2. \$479,150 − \$371,271

3. 612,797 + 811,035

4. 638,113 − 415,327

5. 5,324 + 2,468

6. \$6,372 − \$4,047

7. 721,379 + 150,496

8. \$3,016 − \$2,849

9. 8,492 + 1,346

10. 846,134 − 794,134

11. 461,137 + 91,214

12. 9,263 + 1,489

Write the missing digit for the estimated sum or difference.

13. □46,164 − 471,467 = 100,000 ______

14. 23,497 + □2,464 = 80,000 ______

15. 631,431 − □26,497 = 500,000 ______

16. □79,431 + 231,587 = 400,000 ______

17. □21,863 − 135,632 = 300,000 ______

18. 54,961 + □5,246 = 70,000 ______

19. □45,239 − 232,878 = 100,000 ______

20. 58,138 + □3,245 = 90,000 ______

**Mixed Review**

21. 27 + 49

22. 31 + 64

23. 92 + 11

24. 87 + 34

25. 16 + 77

Name ______________________________



## Subtract Across Zeros

Find the difference. Estimate to check.

1. 3,000 − 2,780
2. 4,003 − 2,232
3. 8,005 − 5,004
4. 6,200 − 4,816
5. 5,700 − 1,751
6. 9,100 − 3,759
7. 20,000 − 13,652
8. 10,000 − 2,842
9. 90,000 − 66,536
10. 50,000 − 13,747
11. 20,000 − 15,136
12. 50,075 − 32,097
13. 70,000 − 29,134
14. 50,000 − 19,673
15. 70,006 − 43,989
16. 20,000 − 9,342

Compare. Write <, >, or = in each ◯.

17. 2,006 − 1,513 ◯ 4,075 − 3,209
18. 7,004 − 6,315 ◯ 5,075 − 4,897
19. 8,003 − 3,695 ◯ 7,473 − 2,127
20. 9,200 − 5,861 ◯ 6,153 − 2,814
21. 3,009 − 1,819 ◯ 8,006 − 6,952
22. 4,284 − 2,651 ◯ 9,000 − 7,367

**Mixed Review**

23. 6,491 + 8,034
24. 9,403 + 199
25. 8,662 + 8,449
26. 7,361 + 9,170
27. 2,649 + 3,427
28. 2,831 + 6,923
29. 1,424 + 3,462
30. $2,455 + $3,119

Name ______________________



# Choose a Method

Find the sum or difference. Estimate to check.

1. 213,742 + 170,045
2. 408,587 − 345,128
3. 248,232 + 236,816
4. 684,004 − 195,751
5. 661,119 − 423,384
6. 358,379 + 264,175
7. 568,075 − 372,097
8. 468,951 + 236,175

Compare. Write <, >, or = in each ○.

9. 561,257 − 346,052 ○ 846,735 − 612,435
10. 257,132 + 153,087 ○ 210,735 + 128,307
11. 976,034 − 780,347 ○ 461,597 − 265,910

Find the missing digit.

12. 4□6,341 − 275,132 = 221,209 ______
13. 682,318 − 248,1□6 = 434,142 ______
14. 945,132 + 153,□02 = 1,098,734 ______

## Mixed Review

Estimate the sum or difference.

15. 6,842 + 2,981 ______
16. 1,132 + 2,074 + 2,596 ______
17. 4,008 − 2,567 ______

18. 6,921 − 4,071 = ______
19. 3,460 − 782 = ______
20. 8,130 − 3,471 = ______
21. 1,197 − 238 = ______

Name ______________________



# Problem Solving Skill

## Estimate or Find Exact Answers

Tell whether an estimate or an exact answer is needed. Solve.

| Item | Price |
|---|---|
| Poster | $5.95 |
| Souvenir Cup | $3.50 |
| Animal Encyclopedia | $10.00 |
| Hat | $7.50 |
| T-shirt | $12.00 |

1. Mitchell bought a hat and a poster. How much change will he get from $20.00?

______________________

2. About how much money does someone need to buy one of each item?

______________________

3. Tracy wants to buy a t-shirt and a souvenir cup. If she has $15.00, does she have enough? Explain your answer.

______________________

4. Maurice had $15.00. He bought a hat. About how much money is left? Is it enough to buy a poster?

______________________

5. Tanisha and Shauna want to share the Animal Encyclopedia. Tanisha has $4.75 and Shauna has $3.25. How much more money do they need to buy the book?

______________________

6. D'Angelo wants to buy lunch for $5.75 and buy a poster and souvenir cup. About how much money should he bring to the zoo?

______________________

## Mixed Review

7. $1.73 + $0.14

8. $10.00 − $ 8.59

9. 6,285 − 3,119

10. 16,212 + 42,080

11. $19.27 + $11.27

12. $3,204 − $2,413

13. 5,320 + 1,375

14. 9,862 − 7,361

15. $3,228 + $4,228

16. 40,000 − 8,613

Name ______________________



# Expressions

## Vocabulary

Complete the sentence.

1. ______________ tell which operation to do first.

2. An ______________ is a part of a number sentence that has numbers and operation signs, but no equal sign.

---

Tell what you would do first.

3. 4 + (8 − 2) ______

4. (16 − 9) + 3 ______

5. 28 + (5 − 2) ______

Find the value of each expression.

6. 5 + (20 − 8) ______

7. 25 − (6 + 11) ______

8. 5 + (45 − 22) ______

9. 55 + (22 − 9) ______

10. (33 − 17) + 14 ______

11. (42 − 33) + 54 ______

12. (13 + 15 + 9) − 22 ______

13. 45 − (22 + 6 + 3) ______

14. (3,827 − 1,294) + 6,782 ______

## Mixed Review

15. 2,112 + 5,899

16. 85,584 − 29,920

17. 50,008 − 28,251

18. 3,804 + 9,156

19. 3,333 − 1,797

20. 47,310 − 19,894

21. 62,809 − 59,345

22. 8,637 − 4,737

Name ______________________



## Use Parentheses

Choose the expression that shows the given value. Write *a* or *b*.

**1.** 17
**a.** (15 − 2) + 4
**b.** 15 − (2 + 4)

______

**2.** 10
**a.** 16 − (8 + 2)
**b.** (16 − 8) + 2

______

**3.** 13
**a.** (72 − 18) + 41
**b.** 72 − (18 + 41)

______

Show where the parentheses should be placed to make the expression equal to the given value.

**4.** 100 − 8 + 4; 96 ______

**5.** 25 − 4 + 8; 13 ______

**6.** 150 − 65 + 13; 72 ______

**7.** 56 − 24 − 13; 19 ______

**8.** 85 − 25 + 13; 73 ______

**9.** 150 − 25 + 37; 88 ______

Find the number that gives the expression a value of 25.

**10.** (15 − 7) + ■ ______

**11.** 50 − (45 − ■) ______

**12.** (31 + ■) − 11 ______

### Mixed Review

**13.** 19 − 8 = ______
11 + 8 = ______

**14.** 6 + 7 = ______
13 − 6 = ______

**15.** 12 − 9 = ______
3 + 9 = ______

Find the missing number.

**16.** 62 + ■ = 89 ______

**17.** 14 + ■ = 33 ______

**18.** 72 − ■ = 46 ______

**19.** ■ − 11 = 89 ______

**20.** ■ + 44 = 74 ______

**21.** ■ + 39 = 106 ______

Name ______________________



# Match Words and Expressions

Choose the expression that matches the words.

1. There were 12 apples in the fruit bowl. Three were eaten and 6 more were added.

   a. 12 − (3 + 6)

   b. (12 − 3) + 6

2. Emily had $22. She spent $6 at the mall and then earned $8 more.

   a. ($22 − $6) + $8

   b. $22 − ($6 + $8)

3. The library has 86 biographies. Seven are checked out and 4 are thrown away.

   a. 86 − (7 + 4)

   b. (86 − 7) + 4

4. Riley had 50¢. She spent 10¢ at the store and played a video game for 25¢.

   a. (50¢ − 10¢) + 25¢

   b. 50¢ − (10¢ + 25¢)

Write an expression for each. Solve.

5. There are 16 people at the Swim Club meeting. 5 people leave and 7 more people come.

   ______________________

6. Rob had 52 baseball cards. He gave 5 to Larry and 8 to Evan.

   ______________________

7. Kari had 10 workbook pages for homework. She did 3 after school and 5 after dinner.

   ______________________

8. Lisa earned $20 doing yard-work. She got a $3 tip and spent $12.

   ______________________

## Mixed Review

9. 63,899 − 47,641

10. 389,290 + 592,921 + 491,911

11. 48,001 − 5,842

12. 493,722 + 891,836 + 105,069

13. (27 + 3 + 9) − 15 ______________________

14. 91 − (42 + 18 + 5) ______________________

15. (6,963 − 280) + 7,118 ______________________

Name ______________________________

LESSON 5.1

# Collect and Organize Data

## Vocabulary

Complete the sentence.

1. The numbers in the ______________________ column show the sum as each new line of data is entered.

For 2–3, use the frequency table.

| FROZEN POPS SOLD | | |
|---|---|---|
| Day | Frequency (Number of Frozen Pops) | Cumulative Frequency |
| Monday | 15 | 15 |
| Tuesday | 24 | 39 |
| Wednesday | 19 | 58 |
| Thursday | 9 | 67 |
| Friday | 21 | 88 |

2. The cumulative frequency for Wednesday is ________. This is the sum of the numbers in the frequency column for which days?

______________, ______________, and ______________.

3. How many frozen pops in all were sold on Monday and Tuesday?

______________________________________________

## Mixed Review

Order the numbers from *greatest* to *least*.

4. 234,358; 23,208; 23,098

______________________

5. 12,214; 342,351; 120,142

______________________

6. 342,253; 34,235; 34,270

______________________

7. 824,723; 8,247; 82,492

______________________

Name ______________________



# Find Median and Mode

## Vocabulary

Complete the sentence.

1. In a group of numbers ordered from the least to the greatest, the number in the middle is called the ____________, and the number that occurs most often is called the ____________.

For 2–5, use the table.

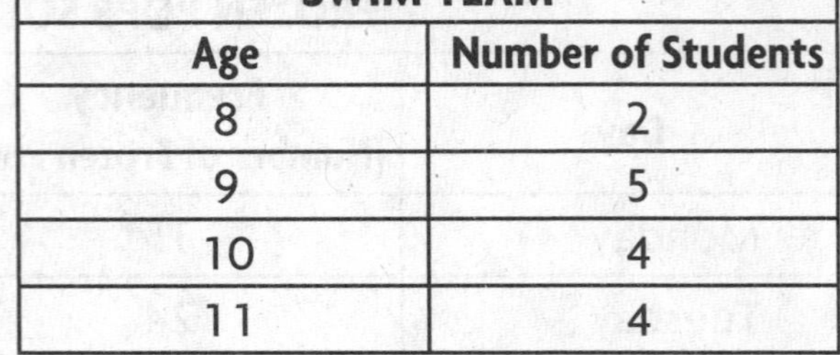

| SWIM TEAM | |
|---|---|
| Age | Number of Students |
| 8 | 2 |
| 9 | 5 |
| 10 | 4 |
| 11 | 4 |

2. List all of the ages of all the swim team members, from least to greatest.

______________________

______________________

3. Use your list from problem 1. What is the median age of the swim team members?

______________________

4. What is the mode of the ages of the swim team members?

______________________

5. What if there were a new swimmer added to the table. Her age is 10. Would that change the mode? Explain.

______________________

______________________

## Mixed Review

Round each number to the nearest hundred.

6. 56,298 ____________
7. 355,207 ____________
8. 514,899 ____________
9. 29,909 ____________
10. 17,923 ____________
11. 99,903 ____________

Find $n$.

12. $4 \times n = 9 + 3$ ____________
13. $n \times 5 = 20 + 5$ ____________
14. $8 + n = 10 + 6$ ____________
15. $5 \times n = 2 \times 10$ ____________
16. $6 + 5 = 9 + n$ ____________
17. $8 \times 2 = n + 9$ ____________
18. $4 \times n = 11 + 1$ ____________
19. $n + 7 = 19 + 12$ ____________

Name ___________________________________



# Line Plot

## Vocabulary

Complete the sentences.

1. A ______________ is a graph that shows data along a number line.
2. The difference between the greatest and the least numbers in a set of data is called the ______________.

---

For 3–4, use the line plot at right.

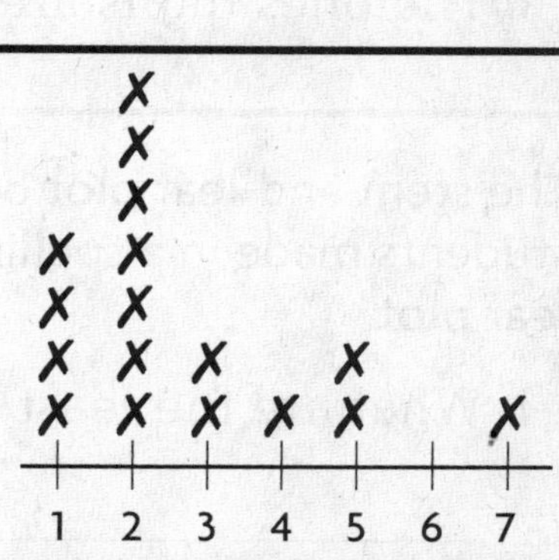


3. The X's on this line plot represent the number of students. What do the numbers on the line plot represent?

   ___________________________________

4. What number of children do more students have in their families?

   ___________________________________

| Slices of Pizza Eaten at a Party | | | | | | |
|---|---|---|---|---|---|---|
| Number of Slices | 0 | 1 | 2 | 3 | 4 | 5 |
| Number of Students | // | ~~////~~ / | ~~////~~ | /// | / | // |

Slices of Pizza Eaten at a Party

5. Use the data in the table to complete the line plot.

## Mixed Review

Write each number in standard form.

6. 100,000 + 50,000 + 4,000

   ___________________________________

7. ninety-six thousand

   ___________________________________

8. nine hundred seventy thousand, eight hundred fifty-two

   ___________________________________

9. 400,000 + 80 + 8

   ___________________________________

Name ______________________



# Stem-and-Leaf Plot

## Vocabulary

Complete the sentences.

1. A ______________ shows groups of data organized by place value.
2. Each tens digit is called a ______________.
3. The ones digits are called the ______________.

---

The stem-and-leaf plot below shows the scores that fourth-grade students made in a spelling contest. For 4–6, use the stem-and-leaf plot.

4. What are the least and the greatest scores?

______________

5. What is the mode of the contest scores?

______________

6. What is the median of the contest scores?

______________

**Spelling Scores**

| Stem | Leaves |
|---|---|
| 6 | 8 8 9 9 |
| 7 | 2 3 5 5 6 |
| 8 | 4 4 6 7 8 8 8 |
| 9 | 1 2 2 3 4 5 5 |

6|8 = 68

## Mixed Review

Find the value of *n*.

7. $5 \times 6 = n$ ______
8. $9 \times 4 = n$ ______
9. $6 \times 9 = n$ ______
10. $n - 3 = 4$ ______
11. $7 + 12 = n$ ______
12. $63 \div n = 9$ ______
13. $10 + n = 13$ ______
14. $7 \times n = 56$ ______
15. $8 \times n = 64$ ______
16. Round 39,457 to the nearest 10,000.

______________

17. Ted bought eggs for \$1.98, milk for \$2.19, and bread for \$1.10. What change should he receive from \$10.00? ______________

Name ______________________



# Compare Graphs

## Vocabulary

Complete the sentence.

1. The ______________ is the series of numbers placed at fixed distances on the side of a graph.

2. The ______________ of a graph is the difference between any two numbers on the scale.

---

For 3–6, use the graph.

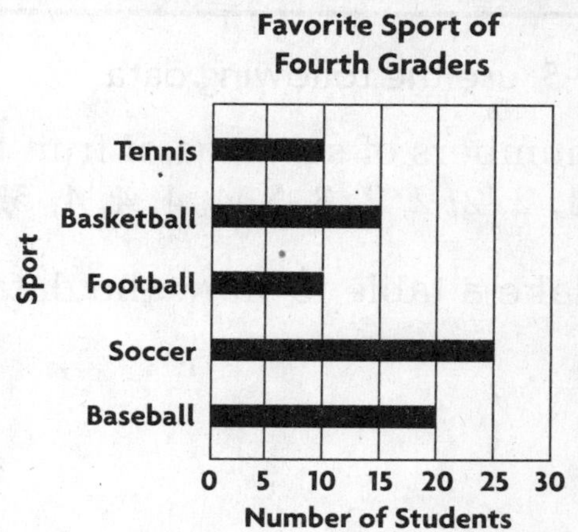


3. What is the interval of the scale in the graph?

______________

4. How would the bars change in the graph if the interval were 1?

______________

5. Describe how the bars in the graph would look if you made a new graph, using a scale interval of 10.

______________

6. Suppose the scale of a bar graph is 0, 4, 8, 12, 16, 20. Describe the bar length that would represent the number 10.

______________

______________

## Mixed Review

7. 55 + 23 ______ 8. 44 − 23 ______ 9. 12 + 34 ______ 10. 87 + 12 ______

11. 5 × 6 ______ 12. 72 ÷ 9 ______ 13. 12 × 12 ______ 14. 45 ÷ 5 ______

15. A baker can make 8 batches of cookies an hour. How many batches of cookies can the baker make in 7 hours?

______________

16. Kim has a scarf. It has a red stripe, a blue stripe, then a white stripe. This pattern repeats. What color is the eighth stripe?

______________

Name ______________________



# Problem Solving Strategy

## Make a Graph

### Vocabulary

Complete the sentences.

1. We can use a ______________ to help see information more easily.

2. Two types of graphs or plots are: ______________________________

______________________________________________

For 3–5, use the following data.

The numbers of servings of fruit the students ate in one day were
1, 1, 1, 2, 2, 2, 2, 3, 3, 4, 4, 4, 4, 5.

3. Make a table to show the data.

4. Make a bar graph of the data.

5. Make a line plot of the data.



### Mixed Review

6. Find the mode of these numbers.
14, 14, 15, 16, 18, 18, 18, 20, 22. ______________

7. $12.75 + $13.22 ______________

8. $34 \times 3$ ______________

Name ______________________

# Problem Solving Skill

## Draw Conclusions

For 1–7, use the graph.

The parents of Mrs. Watkins' fourth grade students wanted to compare their favorite music choices for the Academic Dinner. Mr. Kennedy took a survey and made a double-bar graph.

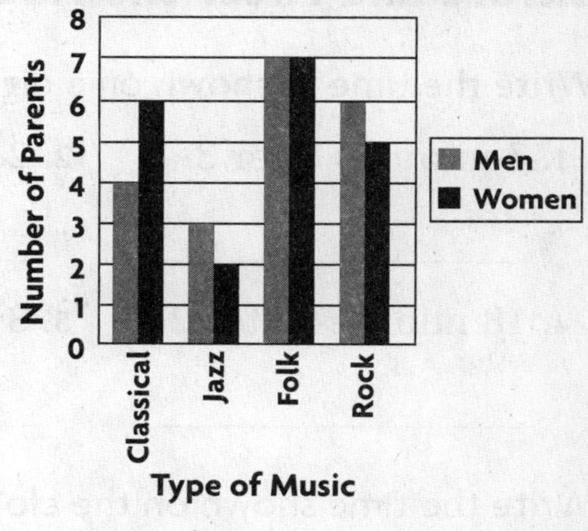


1. What is the favorite music choice for men?

2. What is the favorite music choice for women?

3. How many men prefer to have rock music at the banquet?

4. How many women prefer classical music?

5. Which type of music is preferred equally by the men and women?

6. How many men were surveyed altogether? women?

7. Is it reasonable to conclude that the parents chose folk music for the Academic Dinner? Explain.

### Mixed Review

8. What number is 100,000 greater than 3,489,234?

9. Round 355,790 to the nearest thousand.

10. Estimate. 390,645 + 71,960

11. Estimate. 495,931 + 889,853

Name ______________________



# Before and After the Hour

Write the time as shown on a digital clock.

1. 7 minutes after 3 ______
2. 28 minutes before 11 ______
3. 15 minutes after 5 ______
4. 18 minutes after 2 ______
5. 3 minutes after 12 ______
6. 15 minutes before 7 ______

Write the time shown on the clock in 2 different ways.

7. 

______
______
______

8. 

______
______
______

9. 

______
______
______

Write the letter of the unit used to measure the time.
Use each answer only once.

10. to take a shower ______
11. to drive across the United States ______
12. to button a button ______
13. to get a night's sleep ______

a. days
b. hours
c. minutes
d. seconds

## Mixed Review

14. Find the value of the expression.
59 − (32 + 12) ______

15. Find the value of the expression.
(28 − 9) − (4 + 8) ______

16. Order from least to greatest:
37,623; 37,326; 36,723

______

17. Estimate the difference
between 47,791 and 35,167.

______

Name ______________________



# A.M. and P.M.

## Vocabulary

Complete.

1. ________ means "before noon."

2. ________ means "after noon."

---

Write the time, using A.M. or P.M.

3. when the sun rises ________

4. when you eat dinner ________

5. when school starts ________

6. when the gas station closes ________

7. when you eat breakfast ________

8. when the mall opens ________

Write A.M. or P.M.

9. Marty has a doctor's appointment at 11:15 ________.

10. Ron is going shopping from 3 ________ to 5 ________.

11. Marci is baby-sitting at 9:30 Saturday morning ________.

12. Juan's shift begins at 4:45 in the afternoon ________.

## Mixed Review

Find the value of each expression.

13. 45 + (16 − 8) ______

14. 73 − (36 + 23) ______

15. Manuela has 2 one dollar bills, 5 quarters, 8 dimes, a nickel and 3 pennies. How much money does she have?

________________

16. Write five million, six hundred thirty thousand, eight hundred ninety-two in standard form.

________________

Name ____________________



# Elapsed Time

## Vocabulary

Complete the sentence.

1. ____________________ is the time that passes from the start of an activity to the end of that activity.

---

Find the elapsed time.

2. **start:** 7:30 A.M. **end:** 3:30 P.M.

____________

3. **start:** 8:05 A.M. **end:** 9:55 A.M.

____________

4. **start:** 9:12 P.M. **end:** 11:28 P.M.

____________

Complete the table.

| | Start Time | End Time | Elapsed Time |
|---|---|---|---|
| 5. | 7:20 A.M. | | 1 hr 30 min |
| 6. | 10:12 A.M. | 4:15 P.M. | |

For 7–8, use the tour schedule.

| TOURS OF NEW YORK CITY | |
|---|---|
| Tours last about 4 hours and 15 minutes. | |
| **Bus** | **Departure Time** |
| Red Coach | 9:45 A.M. |
| Blue Coach | 11:25 A.M. |
| Green Coach | 1:40 P.M. |
| Yellow Coach | 3:05 P.M. |

7. At about what time does each tour end?

____________________

8. The Gutierrez family is seeing a Broadway show at 5:30 P.M. Which tour(s) can they take?

____________________

## Mixed Review

Find the sum or difference. Estimate to check.

9. 455,967 + 396,128

10. 320,051 − 198,489

11. 4,938,920 + 9,938,593

Name ______________________________

## Problem Solving Skill

### Sequence Information

Mr. Anderson is taking his history class to a museum. The students will take a tour, view 2 movies, and visit the costume room. The bus will drop the class off at 9:15 A.M. and pick them up at 3:30 P.M. Lunch will be from 12:15 P.M. to 12:45 P.M. Tours of the museum last 1 hour and 15 minutes.

| Revolutionary Heroes Movie | |
|---|---|
| running time: 45 min | |
| 9:00 A.M. | 1:00 P.M. |
| 10:00 A.M. | 2:00 P.M. |
| 11:00 A.M. | 3:00 P.M. |

| Battlegrounds Movie | |
|---|---|
| running time: 37 min | |
| 9:30 A.M. | 1:30 P.M. |
| 10:30 A.M. | 2:30 P.M. |
| 11:30 A.M. | 5:00 P.M. |

1. Will the class be able to see both movies before lunch? If so, name a schedule.

______________________________

______________________________

______________________________

______________________________

2. If the class begins the museum tour at 9:40 A.M., will it be able to see *Revolutionary Heroes* and still be ready for lunch at 12:15 P.M.? Explain.

______________________________

______________________________

______________________________

3. If the class visits the costume room at 1:45 P.M. and stays for one hour and 10 minutes, can it view *Revolutionary Heroes* and be ready to meet the bus?

______________________________

______________________________

______________________________

4. Make a schedule for the class which includes both movies, a tour of the museum, and a visit to the costume room.

| My Museum Tour Schedule | |
|---|---|
| | |
| | |
| | |
| Lunch | 12:15 P.M.–12:45 P.M. |
| | |
| | |
| | |

## Mixed Review

5. 370,716 − 192,408

6. 971,858 − 863,245

7. 4,330,629 + 6,197,550

8. 3,606,117 − 3,432,980

Name ______________________



# Elapsed Time on a Calendar

For 1–3, use the calendars.

| Camp Windy | |
|---|---|
| Session 1: | Jul 13–Jul 17 |
| Session 2: | Jul 27–Jul 31 |
| Session 3: | Aug 3–Aug 14 |

**June**

| Sun | Mon | Tue | Wed | Thu | Fri | Sat |
|---|---|---|---|---|---|---|
| | 1 | 2 | 3 | 4 | 5 | 6 |
| 7 | 8 | 9 | 10 | 11 | 12 | 13 |
| 14 | 15 | 16 | 17 | 18 | 19 | 20 |
| 21 | 22 | 23 | 24 | 25 | 26 | 27 |
| 28 | 29 | 30 | | | | |

**July**

| Sun | Mon | Tue | Wed | Thu | Fri | Sat |
|---|---|---|---|---|---|---|
| | | | 1 | 2 | 3 | 4 |
| 5 | 6 | 7 | 8 | 9 | 10 | 11 |
| 12 | 13 | 14 | 15 | 16 | 17 | 18 |
| 19 | 20 | 21 | 22 | 23 | 24 | 25 |
| 26 | 27 | 28 | 29 | 30 | 31 | |

**August**

| Sun | Mon | Tue | Wed | Thu | Fri | Sat |
|---|---|---|---|---|---|---|
| | | | | | | 1 |
| 2 | 3 | 4 | 5 | 6 | 7 | 8 |
| 9 | 10 | 11 | 12 | 13 | 14 | 15 |
| 16 | 17 | 18 | 19 | 20 | 21 | 22 |
| 23 | 24 | 25 | 26 | 27 | 28 | 29 |
| 30 | 31 | | | | | |

**1.** The camp director bought art supplies 4 weeks before the beginning of the first session of camp. On what date did she buy art supplies?

______________________

**2.** In Session 3, the campers put on a puppet show on the second Wednesday of the session. What was the date of the puppet show?

______________________

**3.** Jim plans to attend Session 2 of camp. His last day of school is June 19. About how many weeks of summer vacation will Jim have before camp begins?

______________________

## Mixed Review

Find the value of each expression.

**4.** $125 - (65 + 22)$ ______________

**5.** $234 - (24 - 13)$ ______________

**6.** $4,590 - (1,293 - 389)$ ______________

Round to the nearest ten thousand.

**7.** 472,099 ______________

**8.** 939,658 ______________

**9.** 3,514,811 ______________

Name ______________________



# Relate Multiplication and Division

Find the value of the variable. Write a related equation.

**1.** $21 \div 3 = t$

**2.** $5 \times 5 = c$

**3.** $16 \div 2 = a$

**4.** $18 \div 6 = d$

**5.** $54 \div 9 = k$

**6.** $4 \times 4 = b$

**7.** $6 \times 2 = f$

**8.** $35 \div 7 = h$

**9.** $8 \div n = 2$

**10.** $4 \times p = 24$

**11.** $30 \div z = 6$

**12.** $6 \times j = 48$

**13.** $g \div 7 = 8$

**14.** $y \div 1 = 6$

**15.** $k \times 6 = 42$

**16.** $n \times 7 = 63$

Write the fact family for each set of numbers.

**17.** 3, 4, 12

**18.** 4, 7, 28

**19.** 5, 10, 50

**20.** 8, 9, 72

## Mixed Review

**21.**
$11.21
$12.15
+$ 1.61

**22.**
1,242,316
− 164,320

**23.**
6,548,957
3,847,200
+ 9,874,512

**24.**
$15.27
$ 7.99
+$ 3.25

**25.** 8 ×8

**26.** 9 ×4

**27.** 6 ×7

**28.** 3 ×5

**29.** 7 ×8

Name ______________________________



# Multiply and Divide Facts Through 5

Find a related multiplication or division equation.

**1.** $2 \times 4 = 8$

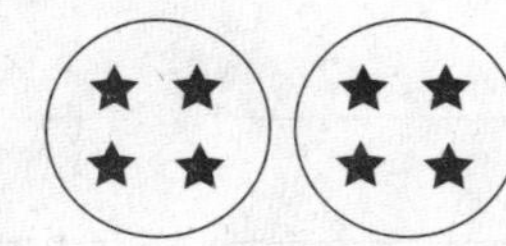

______________________

**2.** $2 \times 5 = 10$

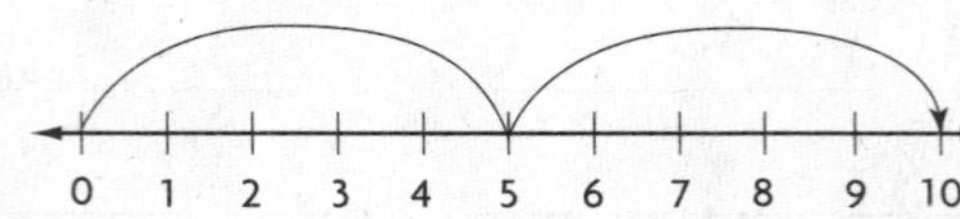


______________________

**3.** $2 \times 2 = 4$

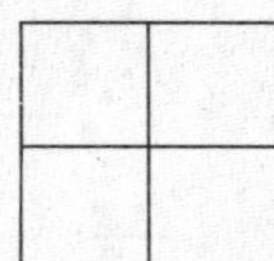

______________________

**4.** $4 \times 1 = 4$

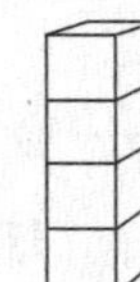

______________________

Find the product or quotient.

**5.** $6 \times 2$ ________

**6.** $21 \div 7$ ________

**7.** $9 \times 5$ ________

**8.** $28 \div 4$ ________

**9.** $8 \times 3$ ________

**10.** $24 \div 6$ ________

**11.** $18 \div 2$ ________

**12.** $5 \times 8$ ________

Find the value of the variable.

**13.** $7 \times 2 = 14$, so $(7 \times 2) + 10 = r$.

______________________

**14.** $(36 \div 4) = 9$, so $(36 \div 4) \times 5 = m$.

______________________

Write $<$, $>$, or $=$ in each ◯.

**15.** $27 \div 3$ ◯ $2 \times 4$

**16.** $32 \div 4$ ◯ $3 \times 3$

**Mixed Review**

**17.** Find the value. $(22 - 6) + 38$

______________________

**18.** In the number 1,257,863 what digit is in the ten thousands place?

______________________

Name ______________________ 

# Multiply and Divide Facts Through 10

Show how the arrays can be used to find the product.

**1.** What is 7 × 8?

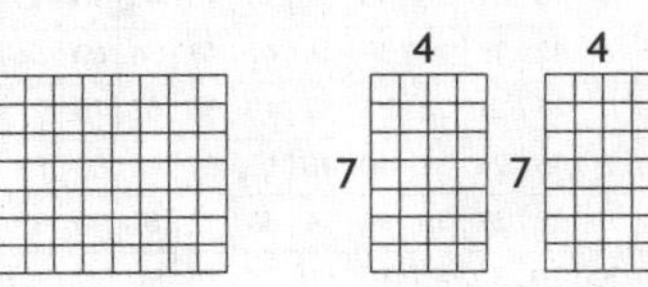


7 × 4 = __________

7 × 4 = __________

So, 7 × 8 = __________.

**2.** What is 6 × 8?

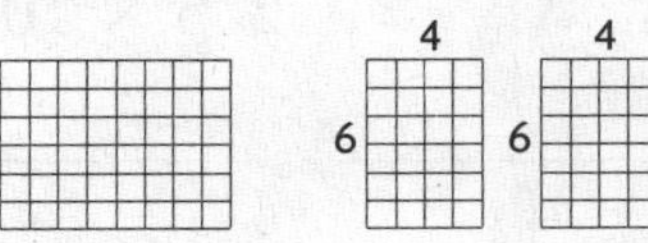


6 × 4 = __________

6 × 4 = __________

So, 6 × 8 = __________.

Find the product or quotient. Show the strategy you used.

**3.** 6 × 6 __________

**4.** 56 ÷ 7 __________

**5.** 8 × 5 __________

**6.** 36 ÷ 4 __________

**7.** 10 × 6 __________

**8.** 72 ÷ 8 __________

**9.** 9 × 7 __________

**10.** 56 ÷ 8 __________

**11.** 8 × 6 __________

**12.** 42 ÷ 6 __________

**13.** 90 ÷ 9 __________

**14.** 9 × 9 __________

**15.** 7 × 6 __________

**16.** 8 × 9 __________

**17.** 49 ÷ 7 __________

**18.** 54 ÷ 9 __________

## Mixed Review

**19.** In the number 125,588,325 what digit is in the ten millions place?

__________

**20.** Find the elapsed time.
Start: 7:54 A.M. End: 9:12 P.M.

__________

**21.** Round 362,847,321 to the nearest million.

__________

**22.** Round 13,567 to the nearest hundred.

__________

**23.** Write an expression using the variable $n$. There were 9 pears in the bowl. Jenny took some out.

__________

**24.** Write an equation using the variable $p$. Ed had some pens. He gave Ben 6 and now has 12.

__________

Name ______________________



# Multiplication Table Through 12

| × | 0 | 1 | 2 | 3 | 4 | 5 | 6 | 7 | 8 | 9 | 10 | 11 | 12 |
|---|---|---|---|---|---|---|---|---|---|---|---|---|---|
| 0 | 0 | 0 | 0 | 0 | 0 | 0 | 0 | 0 | 0 | 0 | 0 | 0 | 0 |
| 1 | 0 | 1 | 2 | 3 | 4 | 5 | 6 | 7 | 8 | 9 | 10 | 11 | 12 |
| 2 | 0 | 2 | 4 | 6 | 8 | 10 | 12 | 14 | 16 | 18 | 20 | 22 | 24 |
| 3 | 0 | 3 | 6 | 9 | 12 | 15 | 18 | 21 | 24 | 27 | 30 | 33 | 36 |
| 4 | 0 | 4 | 8 | 12 | 16 | 20 | 24 | 28 | 32 | 36 | 40 | 44 | 48 |
| 5 | 0 | 5 | 10 | 15 | 20 | 25 | 30 | 35 | 40 | 45 | 50 | 55 | 60 |
| 6 | 0 | 6 | 12 | 18 | 24 | 30 | 36 | 42 | 48 | 54 | 60 | 66 | 72 |
| 7 | 0 | 7 | 14 | 21 | 28 | 35 | 42 | 49 | 56 | 63 | 70 | 77 | 84 |
| 8 | 0 | 8 | 16 | 24 | 32 | 40 | 48 | 56 | 64 | 72 | 80 | 88 | 96 |
| 9 | 0 | 9 | 18 | 27 | 36 | 45 | 54 | 63 | 72 | 81 | 90 | 99 | 108 |
| 10 | 0 | 10 | 20 | 30 | 40 | 50 | 60 | 70 | 80 | 90 | 100 | 110 | 120 |
| 11 | 0 | 11 | 22 | 33 | 44 | 55 | 66 | 77 | 88 | 99 | 110 | 121 | 132 |
| 12 | 0 | 12 | 24 | 36 | 48 | 60 | 72 | 84 | 96 | 108 | 120 | 132 | 144 |

Use the multiplication table to find the product or quotient.

**1.** $40 \div 4$ ______ **2.** $5 \times 10$ ______

**3.** $70 \div 10$ ______ **4.** $110 \div 10$ ______

**5.** $11 \div 1$ ______ **6.** $10 \times 8$ ______ **7.** $12 \times 12$ ______ **8.** $66 \div 11$ ______

**9.** $7 \times 12$ ______ **10.** $108 \div 9$ ______ **11.** $11 \times 5$ ______ **12.** $36 \div 3$ ______

Find the value of the variable.

**13.** $30 \div 10 = t$ ______ **14.** $121 \div y = 11$ ______ **15.** $80 \div 8 = h$ ______ **16.** $n \times 12 = 48$ ______

**17.** $k \times 11 = 132$ ______ **18.** $10 \times p = 100$ ______ **19.** $72 \div z = 6$ ______ **20.** $11 \times j = 99$ ______

**Mixed Review**

**21.** $63 + $48 + $122

______

**22.** Write one thousand, eighty-five in standard form.

______

**23.** In 7,894,132, what digit is in the ten thousands place?

______

**24.** Round 63,947 to the nearest ten.

______

**25.** Find the median.
15, 18, 22, 11, 20, 20, 13

______

**26.** Find the mode.
15, 18, 22, 11, 20, 20, 13

______

**27.** $(14 - 8) + 17 =$ ______

**28.** $36 - (3 + 9) =$ ______

**29.** $(15 + 15) - (12 + 2) =$ ______

**30.** $(17 - 6) + (42 - 17) =$ ______

Name ______________________

# Multiply 3 Factors

Find the product.

1. $3 \times (2 \times 4)$ ______
2. $10 \times (2 \times 6)$ ______
3. $(6 \times 5) \times 0$ ______
4. $8 \times (2 \times 6)$ ______
5. $8 \times (1 \times 7)$ ______
6. $6 \times (3 \times 2)$ ______
7. $(2 \times 6) \times 2$ ______
8. $(2 \times 3) \times 9$ ______
9. $(3 \times 4) \times 9$ ______
10. $(3 \times 4) \times 4$ ______
11. $(3 \times 3) \times 3$ ______
12. $10 \times (5 \times 2)$ ______

Show two ways to group by using parentheses. Find the product.

13. $11 \times 1 \times 5$ ______
14. $4 \times 2 \times 6$ ______
15. $2 \times 6 \times 1$ ______
16. $2 \times 4 \times 3$ ______

Write <, >, or = in each ○.

17. $(1 \times 9) \times 6$ ○ $3 \times (6 \times 2)$
18. $(6 \times 2) \times 3$ ○ $4 \times (3 \times 3)$
19. $3 \times 4 \times 3$ ○ $9 \times 2 \times 2$
20. $(6 \times 2) \times 6$ ○ $11 \times (4 \times 3)$

## Mixed Review

21. In the number 25,327, what digit is in the thousands place? ______
22. Round 8,569 to the nearest hundred. ______
23. (\$7,321 − \$1,435) + \$2,600 ______
24. (4,828 + 179) − 3,990 ______

Name ____________________



# Problem Solving Skill

## Choose the Operation

Solve. Name the operation or operations you used.

1. Kate sold 21 boxes of cookies. Randy sold 32 boxes of cookies. Gina sold 49 boxes of cookies. How many boxes did they sell?

   ____________________

2. Behind home plate there are 5 rows of seats. Each row has 7 seats in it. How many seats are in this section?

   ____________________

3. The pottery classroom has 3 tables. There are 6 people at each table. If each person makes 2 clay animals, how many clay animals are made?

   ____________________

4. The fine for an overdue book at the Cotter Library is 5¢ a day. Tyler returned his books 1 day late. He paid a 30¢ fine. How many books did he return?

   ____________________

5. Ashley, Suzanne and Liz bought a box of chocolates. There are 36 chocolates in the box. How many do they get each?

   ____________________

6. Clyde sleeps 8 hours each night. How many hours does he sleep each week?

   ____________________

7. On Tuesday morning, Mrs. Corbett drove 57 miles to Princeton. Then she drove to Natick. She drove a total of 90 miles. How many miles was it from Princeton to Natick?

   ____________________

8. Peter took a three-day 28-mile backpacking trip. He hiked 9 miles the first day and 11 miles the second day. How many miles did he hike the third day?

   ____________________

## Mixed Review

9. Find the median.
   546, 550, 420, 410, 560, 530, 530

   ____________________

10. Find the mode.
    546, 550, 420, 410, 560, 530, 530

    ____________________

11. In the number 12,482 what digit is in the tens place?

    ____________________

12. What is the elapsed time between 9:27 A.M. and 6:32 P.M.?

    ____________________

Name ____________________

# Expressions with Parentheses

Find the value of the expression.

1. $(49 - 22) \div 3$ ________
2. $88 - (12 \times 4)$ ________
3. $14 + (6 \times 9)$ ________
4. $123 - (45 \div 5)$ ________
5. $(42 \div 7) \times 8$ ________
6. $3 \times (4 + 8)$ ________
7. $(55 - 35) \div 5$ ________
8. $55 - (35 \div 5)$ ________
9. $34 + (27 \div 9)$ ________
10. $36 \div (4 + 5)$ ________
11. $155 - (81 \div 9)$ ________
12. $7 \times (25 \div 5)$ ________

Choose the expression that shows the given value.

13. 55
    a. $(9 \times 6) + 1$
    b. $9 \times (6 + 1)$

14. 70
    a. $7 \times (3 + 7)$
    b. $(7 \times 3) + 7$

15. 12
    a. $(2 \times 8) - 2$
    b. $2 \times (8 - 2)$

Find the value of the expression.

16. $(243 - 124) - (4 \times 5)$ ________
17. $(15 \div 3) \times (22 - 14)$ ________
18. $(14 \div 2) \times (44 - 33)$ ________
19. $(7 \times 4) + (18 \div 2)$ ________

## Mixed Review

Solve.

20. $9 \times 6$
21. $5 \times 12$
22. $7 \times 8$
23. $10 \times 6$
24. $5 \times 8$
25. $12 \times 7$
26. $4 \times 11$
27. $9 \times 5$
28. $8 \times 8$
29. $6 \times 7$

Name ______________________________



# Match Words and Expressions

Choose the expression that matches the words.

1. Ali had $9 and then worked 3 hours for $6 per hour.

   a. (9 + 3) × 6

   b. 9 + (3 × 6)

2. Jane had 57¢. She lost 2 dimes.

   a. (57 − 2) × 10

   b. 57 − (2 × 10)

3. Larry had 12 books. Eleven of the books had 10 pages each. The twelfth book had 15 pages.

   a. (10 × 11) + 15

   b. 10 × (11 + 15)

4. Rashid had 16 pens. Nine were broken, then Rashid bought a package that doubled the number of pens he had left.

   a. (16 − 9) × 2

   b. 16 − (9 × 2)

5. Jeff bought 5 models which each cost $7. He paid $2 in sales tax.

   a. (5 × 2) + 7

   b. (5 × 7) + 2

6. Mr. Gibson's band room has 8 rows of 6 chairs each. There are also 3 chairs not in rows.

   a. (8 × 6) + 3

   b. (3 × 6) + 8

7. Eloise planted 6 rows of tulips with 5 plants in each row. She put 3 more plants in another row.

   a. (6 × 5) + 3

   b. 6 × (5 + 3)

8. Joel built 3 birdhouses each day for a week and then the dog knocked over and broke 2 of the birdhouses.

   a. (3 × 2) − 7

   b. (3 × 7) − 2

## Mixed Review

Find the value of the expression.

9. (5 + 6) − (3 + 4) ______________

10. 15 − (27 − 14) ______________

11. (2 × 6) ÷ 4 ______________

12. 9,002 − 8,008

13. 7,958 + 1,798

14. 4,621 + 3,299

Name ______________________________



# Equations with Variables

Choose the equation that matches the words.

1. The number of dollars, $d$, divided evenly by 6 people is 4.

   a. $d \div 4 = 6$ b. $d \div 6 = 4$
   c. $6 \div 4 = d$ d. $4 \div 6 = d$

2. The number of plants, $p$, on 8 shelves is 32.

   a. $p \div 8 = 32$ b. $8 \div p = 32$
   c. $p \times 8 = 32$ d. $32 \times p = 8$

Write an equation for each. Choose a variable for the unknown. Tell what the variable represents.

3. 6 bicycles in each of 6 rows is the total number of bicycles.

   ______________________________

   ______________________________

4. Some number of plants in each of 7 rows is 84 plants.

   ______________________________

   ______________________________

5. 12 ounces of water in each of a number of bottles is 60 ounces of water.

   ______________________________

   ______________________________

6. 72 marbles divided evenly among 8 bags is some number of marbles in each bag.

   ______________________________

   ______________________________

7. A number of pencils divided equally among 5 boxes is 9 pencils in each box.

   ______________________________

   ______________________________

8. 25 books divided evenly among some number of students is 5 books per student.

   ______________________________

   ______________________________

## Mixed Review

9. Round 1,793,445 to the nearest million.

   ______________________________

10. Round 1,428,739 to the nearest hundred thousand.

   ______________________________

11. $12 \times 9 = n$ ____________

12. $144 \div 12 = n$ ____________

13. $90 \div h = 9$ ____________

Name ______________________

# Find a Rule

Find a rule. Write the rule as an equation.

**1.**

| Input | Output |
|---|---|
| *a* | *b* |
| 15 | 3 |
| 20 | 4 |
| 25 | 5 |
| 30 | 6 |

**2.**

| Input | Output |
|---|---|
| *c* | *d* |
| 4 | 16 |
| 5 | 20 |
| 6 | 24 |
| 7 | 28 |

**3.**

| Input | Output |
|---|---|
| *s* | *t* |
| 2 | 16 |
| 3 | 24 |
| 4 | 32 |
| 5 | 40 |

**4.**

| Input | Output |
|---|---|
| *p* | *r* |
| 5 | 35 |
| 6 | 42 |
| 7 | 49 |
| 8 | 56 |

Use the rule and the equation to make an input/output table.

**5.** Multiply by 2.
$a \times 2 = c$

| Input | Output |
|---|---|
| | |
| | |
| | |
| | |

**6.** Divide by 3.
$r \div 3 = s$

| Input | Output |
|---|---|
| | |
| | |
| | |
| | |

**7.** Multiply by 11.
$p \times 11 = q$

| Input | Output |
|---|---|
| | |
| | |
| | |
| | |

**8.** Divide by 4.
$y \div 4 = z$

| Input | Output |
|---|---|
| | |
| | |
| | |
| | |

## Mixed Review

Find the value of the expression.

**9.** $12 \times 8$

**10.** $99 \div 11$

**11.** $63 - (14 \div 7)$

**12.** What time is 2 hours and 40 minutes after 11:22 A.M.?

**13.** Write the standard form for three hundred thousand, five.

Name ______________________



# Problem Solving Strategy

## Work Backward

Write an equation and *work backward* to solve.

1. Alexander had some nickels in his bank. He added 3 dimes to the bank and then he had 85¢. How many nickels did Alexander have?

______________________

2. Roz is making a quilt. Yesterday she sewed some squares. Today she sewed together 3 rows with 10 squares each. She has sewn a total of 50 squares. How many squares did Roz sew yesterday?

______________________

*Work backward* to solve.

3. Leo folded a sheet of paper in half a certain number of times. When unfolded, the sheet was divided into 8 sections. How many times did Leo fold the paper in half?

______________________

4. Ann is setting a clock. It says 12:00 P.M. She moves the minute hand forward 10 minutes, back 12 minutes, forward 8 minutes, and back some minutes. If the time now reads 12:03 P.M., what was her final move?

______________________

5. Holly is going from her home to the grocery store. To get to the store, she walks 3 blocks west and 2 blocks south. When she leaves the store, she walks 3 blocks east. How many blocks and in what direction should Holly walk to get home?

______________________

6. Amy and Tim are playing a counting game. They are counting to 30. Amy claps when they say a number that can be divided evenly by 3. Tim claps when they say a number that can be divided evenly by 4. On what numbers do they both clap?

______________________



## Mixed Review

7. $3 \times 8$

8. $9 \times 4$

9. $9 \times 9$

10. $12 \times 6$

11. $12 \times 10$

Name ______________________



# Mental Math: Multiplication Patterns

Use a basic fact and a pattern to write each product.

1. a. $5 \times 50$
   b. $5 \times 500$

2. a. $9 \times 80$
   b. $9 \times 800$

3. a. $2 \times 3{,}000$
   b. $2 \times 30{,}000$

4. a. $9 \times 20$
   b. $9 \times 200$

5. a. $7 \times 9{,}000$
   b. $7 \times 90{,}000$

6. a. $4 \times 4{,}000$
   b. $4 \times 40{,}000$

Multiply mentally. Write the basic multiplication fact and the product.

7. $5 \times 700$
8. $9 \times 400$
9. $9 \times 900$
10. $4 \times 500$
11. $3 \times 4{,}000$
12. $8 \times 3{,}000$

Find the value of *n*.

13. $6 \times 40{,}000 = n$
14. $n = 3 \times 600$
15. $n \times 500 = 3{,}500$
16. $3 \times n = 15{,}000$
17. $n \times 8 = 640$
18. $7 \times n = 42{,}000$
19. $7{,}000 \times n = 49{,}000$
20. $6 \times n = 5{,}400$
21. $n \times 6 = 1{,}800$

**Mixed Review**

22. Write the time in words.

23. Write the time in words.

Name ______________________



# Estimate Products

Round one factor. Estimate the product.

1. 512 × 5
2. 93 × 8
3. 1,401 × 7
4. 257 × 3
5. 981 × 7
6. 82 × 4
7. 127 × 9
8. 741 × 9
9. $15.34 × 7 ________
10. 903 × 4 ________
11. 95 × 9 ________
12. 718 × 3 ________
13. 1,209 × 8 ________
14. 657 × 3 ________
15. 55 × 2 ________
16. 9,099 × 4 ________

Choose two factors from the box for each estimated product. You may use each number more than once.

| 309 | 4 | 759 |
|---|---|---|
| 193 | 3 | 7 |

17. ❑ × Δ = 2,100 ________
18. ❑ × Δ = 800 ________
19. ❑ × Δ = 900 ________
20. ❑ × Δ = 2,400 ________
21. ❑ × Δ = 1,200 ________
22. ❑ × Δ = 5,600 ________

## Mixed Review

23. Order the numbers from *least* to *greatest*.

    182; 128; 1,028; 1,082

    ________

24. Round 194,012 to the nearest ten thousand.

    ________

25. Jeremy said the value of 15 − (7 × 2) is 16. Describe his error.

    ________

    ________

26. The cost of a pizza is $12.00. If four people share the cost equally, how much should each pay?

    ________

Name ______________________

LESSON 10.3

# Multiply 2-Digit Numbers

Multiply. Tell which place-vlaue positions need to be regrouped.

1. 29 × 3 = ______
2. 18 × 4 = ______
3. 37 × 5 = ______
4. 96 × 2 = ______
5. 62 × 4 = ______
6. 15 × 9 = ______
7. 50 × 6 = ______
8. 33 × 6 = ______

Find the product. Estimate to check.

9. 2 × 26 ______
10. 3 × 45 ______
11. 7 × 29 ______
12. 9 × 63 ______
13. 3 × 18 ______
14. 8 × 49 ______
15. 6 × 19 ______
16. 3 × 99 ______

Compare. Write <, >, or = in each ○.

17. 5 × 15 ○ 6 × 12
18. 3 × 42 ○ 6 × 21
19. 7 × 22 ○ 8 × 17
20. 9 × 21 ○ 6 × 37
21. 2 × 79 ○ 3 × 24
22. 8 × 23 ○ 4 × 66

## Mixed Review

23. Which is greater, 909,872 or 990,678?

______

24. Round 192,875 to the nearest thousand.

______

25. Find the median.
10, 12, 19, 18, 12, 13, 12

______

26. Find the mean.
33, 36, 39, 45, 29, 58

______

Name ________________________________



# Model Multiplication

Use base-ten blocks to multiply. Record the product.

1. 5 × 503 ________
2. 4 × 108 ________
3. 4 × 122 ________
4. 3 × 206 ________
5. 3 × 211 ________
6. 4 × 127 ________
7. 2 × 514 ________
8. 3 × 324 ________

Multiply. You may wish to use base-ten blocks.

9. 4 × 305 ________
10. 2 × 108 ________
11. 3 × 212 ________
12. 4 × 211 ________
13. 2 × 131 ________
14. 4 × 217 ________
15. 2 × 415 ________
16. 2 × 253 ________

## Mixed Review

17. 12,489 + 1,429
18. 1,227 − 828
19. 45,123 − 5,124
20. 73,711 − 25,609

For 21–24, use the following graph.

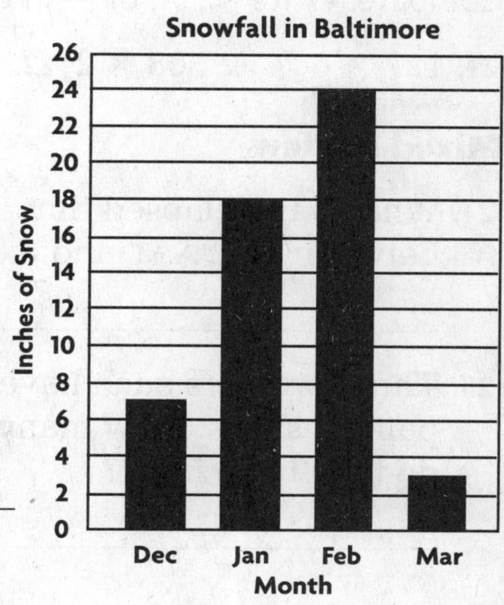


21. What type of graph is shown here? ________

22. How much snow fell in Baltimore during the months of January and February? ________

23. What two months had a total of 31 inches of snowfall? ________

24. What was the total snowfall for all four months? ________

Name ________________________________



# Multiply 3-Digit Numbers

Multiply. Tell which place-value positions need to be regrouped.

1. $\begin{array}{r} 52 \\ \times\ 5 \\ \hline \end{array}$

2. $\begin{array}{r} 83 \\ \times\ 8 \\ \hline \end{array}$

3. $\begin{array}{r} 401 \\ \times\ \ 7 \\ \hline \end{array}$

4. $\begin{array}{r} 207 \\ \times\ \ 3 \\ \hline \end{array}$

5. $\begin{array}{r} 91 \\ \times\ 7 \\ \hline \end{array}$

6. $\begin{array}{r} 862 \\ \times\ \ 4 \\ \hline \end{array}$

7. $\begin{array}{r} 121 \\ \times\ \ 9 \\ \hline \end{array}$

8. $\begin{array}{r} 471 \\ \times\ \ 9 \\ \hline \end{array}$

Find the product. Estimate to check.

9. $504 \times 6$ ____________

10. $230 \times 4$ ____________

11. $59 \times 6$ ____________

12. $812 \times 3$ ____________

13. $29 \times 8$ ____________

14. $57 \times 9$ ____________

15. $755 \times 4$ ____________

16. $929 \times 5$ ____________

17. $\begin{array}{r} 291 \\ \times\ \ 7 \\ \hline \end{array}$ ____________

18. $\begin{array}{r} 82 \\ \times\ 6 \\ \hline \end{array}$ ____________

19. $\begin{array}{r} 517 \\ \times\ \ 9 \\ \hline \end{array}$ ____________

20. $\begin{array}{r} 771 \\ \times\ \ 7 \\ \hline \end{array}$ ____________

Compare. Write $<$, $>$, or $=$ in each ○.

21. $127 \times 6$ ○ $308 \times 2$

22. $94 \times 5$  $57 \times 9$

23. $572 \times 2$  $143 \times 8$

## Mixed Review

24. What is the elapsed time between 5:12 A.M. and 6:05 P.M.?

____________________

25. What is the value of the digit 4 in the number 189.064?

____________________

26. Three brothers each have four pairs of shoes. How many shoes do they have in all?

____________________

27. Write 35,801 in expanded form.

____________________

Name ______________________________



# Multiply 4-Digit Numbers

1. Explain where to put the decimal point in $13.54 × 9.

______________________________

______________________________

Find the product. Estimate to check.

2. 5,092 × 5 ______

3. 834 × 5 ______

4. 4,801 × 3 ______

5. $20.72 × 3 ______

6. $42.91 × 7 ______

7. 6,254 × 7 ______

8. $12.18 × 9 ______

9. $7.81 × 9 ______

10. $46.29 × 3 ______

11. 357 × 6 ______

12. 5,555 × 4 ______

13. $9.24 × 7 ______

14. ($6.94 × 3) × 2 ______

15. (4 × $12.25) × 3 ______

16. (982 × 3) × 7 ______

## Mixed Review

17. If today is July 1, what was yesterday?

______________________________

18. Michele was assigned a project on March 7. If she was given 3 weeks to complete the project, when was it due?

______________________________

19. What is the date two weeks before April 23?

______________________________

20. What is the median number of days in the months of September, October, and November? ______________________________

Name ____________________



# Problem Solving Strategy

## Write an Equation

For 1–5, write an equation and solve.

1. Theresa's father works 5 days a week for 48 weeks a year. How many days does her father work in 1 year?

   ____________________

2. Theresa's father makes $24.50 per hour. How much does he make if he works 8 hours?

   ____________________

3. The football team is raising money for new footballs. How much money does the team need to raise if it wants 6 new footballs and each one costs $17.93?

   ____________________

4. A civil engineer counted the number of cars that passed through an intersection. If 2,457 cars passed through the intersection in one hour, how many cars would pass through the intersection in 8 hours?

   ____________________

5. Brianna practices playing guitar for 60 minutes each day. How many minutes does she practice in one week?

   ____________________

For 6–7, use this information.
Each floor of a nine-story office building has 132 windows.

6. What equation can you use to find the total number of windows?

   A $9 \times n = 132$ C $n \times 132 = 9$

   B $9 \times 132 = n$ D $n \times 9 = 132$

7. How many windows are there in all?

   F 188 H 1,088

   G 881 J 1,188



## Mixed Review

8. $14 \times 5$ 9. $12 \times 8$ 10. $26 \times 3$ 11. $42 \times 2$ 12. $33 \times 5$

13. $2.98 × 7 ____________

14. $14.81 × 3 ____________

Name ______________________________



# Mental Math: Patterns with Multiples

Use a basic fact and a pattern to find the product.

1. $6 \times 5 =$ ____________
   $6 \times 50 =$ ____________
   $6 \times 500 =$ ____________

2. $2 \times 2 =$ ____________
   $2 \times 20 =$ ____________
   $2 \times 200 =$ ____________

3. $3 \times 6 =$ ____________
   $3 \times 60 =$ ____________
   $3 \times 600 =$ ____________
   $3 \times 6{,}000 =$ ____________

4. $9 \times 9 =$ ____________
   $9 \times 90 =$ ____________
   $9 \times 900 =$ ____________
   $9 \times 9{,}000 =$ ____________

5. $10 \times 3 =$ ____________
   $10 \times 30 =$ ____________
   $10 \times 300 =$ ____________
   $10 \times 3{,}000 =$ ____________

6. $40 \times 3 =$ ____________
   $40 \times 30 =$ ____________
   $40 \times 300 =$ ____________
   $40 \times 3{,}000 =$ ____________

7. $600 \times 30 =$ ____________

8. $70 \times 3{,}000 =$ ____________

9. $1{,}000 \times 30 =$ ____________

10. $6{,}000 \times 6{,}000 =$ ____________

Find the value of *n*.

11. $n \times 40 = 8{,}000$

    ____________

12. $900 \times 300 = n$

    ____________

## Mixed Review

Round to the place value of the bold digit.

13. 57,4**0**3,294

    ____________

14. 98**3**,204,448

    ____________

15. **9**82,404

    ____________

Solve.

16. $\begin{array}{r} 300{,}010 \\ -\ 255{,}492 \\ \hline \end{array}$

17. $\begin{array}{r} 392{,}402 \\ 392{,}402 \\ +\ 492{,}148 \\ \hline \end{array}$

18. $\begin{array}{r} 12{,}498 \\ -\ 10{,}816 \\ \hline \end{array}$

Name ______________________________



# Multiply by Multiples of 10

Find the product.

1. $30 \times 5$

2. $60 \times 30$

3. $85 \times 30$

4. $67 \times 90$

5. $30 \times 70$

6. $80 \times 5$

7. $82 \times 50$

8. $95 \times 50$

9. $74 \times 20$ ______

10. $50 \times 48$ ______

11. $60 \times 29$ ______

12. $93 \times 40$ ______

13. $28 \times 50$ ______

14. $72 \times 90$ ______

Find the missing digits.

15. $30 \times$ ___0 $= 300$

16. ___0 $\times 20 = 800$

17. $16 \times$ ___0 $= 640$

18. 4___ $\times 80 = 3{,}600$

19. 1___ $\times 30 = 540$

20. ___4 $\times 50 = 3{,}200$

21. 8___ $\times 20 = 1{,}700$

22. 9___ $\times 60 = 5{,}700$

23. ___6 $\times 80 = 6{,}080$

## Mixed Review

Solve.

24. $n \times 4 = 28$ ______

25. $81 \div b = 9$ ______

26. $t \times (3 \times 2) = 18$ ______

27. $y \times 60 = 420$ ______

28. $300 \times w = 36{,}000$ ______

29. $p \times 500 = 6{,}000$ ______

30. $13 \times 4$

31. $21 \times 5$

32. $17 \times 2$

33. $18 \times 5$

34. $19 \times 3$

35. $25 \times 4$

36. $16 \times 8$

37. $14 \times 7$

Name ______________________



# Estimate Products

Round each factor. Estimate the product.

1. $\begin{array}{r} 35 \\ \times\ 11 \\ \hline \end{array}$
2. $\begin{array}{r} 54 \\ \times\ 32 \\ \hline \end{array}$
3. $\begin{array}{r} 97 \\ \times\ 93 \\ \hline \end{array}$
4. $\begin{array}{r} 549 \\ \times\ 65 \\ \hline \end{array}$
5. $\begin{array}{r} 486 \\ \times\ 74 \\ \hline \end{array}$
6. $\begin{array}{r} 658 \\ \times\ 209 \\ \hline \end{array}$
7. $\begin{array}{r} 648 \\ \times\ 174 \\ \hline \end{array}$
8. $\begin{array}{r} 840 \\ \times\ 151 \\ \hline \end{array}$
9. $\begin{array}{r} 339 \\ \times\ 359 \\ \hline \end{array}$
10. $\begin{array}{r} 884 \\ \times\ 444 \\ \hline \end{array}$
11. $312 \times 45$ ________
12. $951 \times 84$ ________
13. $503 \times 49$ ________
14. $320 \times 40$ ________
15. $39 \times 503$ ________
16. $85 \times 81$ ________
17. $814 \times 242$ ________
18. $957 \times 84$ ________
19. $584 \times 394$ ________
20. $84 \times 315$ ________

Use estimation to compare. Write <, >, or = in each ◯.

21. $609 \times 43$ ◯ 20,000
22. 15,000 ◯ $459 \times 35$
23. $872 \times 254$ ◯ 300,000
24. $965 \times 19$ ◯ 40,000

## Mixed Review

Estimate by rounding to the greatest place value.

25. $\begin{array}{r} 485{,}492 \\ -\ 39{,}492 \\ \hline \end{array}$
26. $\begin{array}{r} 493{,}430 \\ 483{,}582 \\ +\ 7{,}302{,}598 \\ \hline \end{array}$
27. $\begin{array}{r} 361 \\ \times\ 42 \\ \hline \end{array}$
28. $\begin{array}{r} 729 \\ \times\ 58 \\ \hline \end{array}$

Multiply.

29. $\begin{array}{r} 4{,}000 \\ \times\ \ \ 70 \\ \hline \end{array}$
30. $\begin{array}{r} 900 \\ \times\ 300 \\ \hline \end{array}$
31. $\begin{array}{r} 6{,}000 \\ \times\ \ 200 \\ \hline \end{array}$
32. $\begin{array}{r} 3{,}200 \\ \times\ \ \ 20 \\ \hline \end{array}$

Name ______________________________

# Model Multiplication

Make a model, record, and solve.

1. $\begin{array}{r} 16 \\ \times 22 \\ \hline \end{array}$

2. $\begin{array}{r} 24 \\ \times 13 \\ \hline \end{array}$

3. $\begin{array}{r} 19 \\ \times 12 \\ \hline \end{array}$

4. $\begin{array}{r} 25 \\ \times 18 \\ \hline \end{array}$

5. $\begin{array}{r} 15 \\ \times 21 \\ \hline \end{array}$

6. $\begin{array}{r} 20 \\ \times 16 \\ \hline \end{array}$

7. $\begin{array}{r} 14 \\ \times 12 \\ \hline \end{array}$

8. $\begin{array}{r} 25 \\ \times 13 \\ \hline \end{array}$

Make a model to find the product. You may use grid paper and markers.

9. $13 \times 18$ ______

10. $23 \times 15$ ______

11. $62 \times 21$ ______

**Mixed Review**

12. $15 \times 90 = n$ ______

13. $40 \times n = 160{,}000$ ______

14. Order from *greatest* to *least*: 87,433; 86,999; 86,302; 87,593; 87,309 ______

15. What day is 12 days after Wednesday, March 15? ______

Complete the table.

16.

| × | 4 | 12 | 3 | 6 | 5 | 11 | 8 |
|---|---|---|---|---|---|---|---|
| 7 | | | | | | | |
| 9 | | | | | | | |

Name ______________________________



# Problem Solving Strategy

## Solve a Simpler Problem

Break the problem into simpler parts and solve.

1. $40 \times 28 = (40 \times 20) + (40 \times 8)$
   $= \_\_\_\_ + \_\_\_\_$
   $= \_\_\_\_$

2. $80 \times 49 = (\_\_\_\_ \times \_\_\_\_) +$
   $(\_\_\_\_ \times \_\_\_\_)$
   $= \_\_\_\_ + \_\_\_\_$
   $= \_\_\_\_$

A warehouse has many pieces of wood in stock. It is going to sell 312 bundles of wood with 20 pieces of wood in each bundle. How many pieces of wood will be sold?

3. Write an expression to help you solve the problem.

   ______________________

4. Find the total number of pieces of wood sold.

   ______________________

During a bad storm, Benny is using candles for light. He has 30 candles and each one burns for about 115 minutes. About how many minutes of light will the candles give Benny?

5. Write an expression to help you solve the problem.

   ______________________

6. Find the number of minutes of light in 30 candles.

   ______________________

## Mixed Review

7. Mr. Rawlins has 57 fifth graders in his classes. He gives them a test with 30 questions on it. How many answers will he have to read to grade papers?

   ______________________

8. Antoin has $12.50. He wants to buy 20 pens that cost 80¢ each. Does he have enough money?

   ______________________

   ______________________

9. $(13 + 2) \times n = 60$

   ______________

10. $12 - (3 \times 3) = y$

   ______________

11. $(42 - 22) + x = 31$

   ______________

Name ______________________



## Multiply by 2-Digit Numbers

Use regrouping or partial products to find the product. Estimate to check.

1. $\begin{array}{r} 62 \\ \times 35 \\ \hline \end{array}$

2. $\begin{array}{r} 55 \\ \times 29 \\ \hline \end{array}$

3. $\begin{array}{r} 73 \\ \times 44 \\ \hline \end{array}$

4. $\begin{array}{r} 48 \\ \times 27 \\ \hline \end{array}$

5. $\begin{array}{r} 81 \\ \times 17 \\ \hline \end{array}$

6. $\begin{array}{r} 67 \\ \times 23 \\ \hline \end{array}$

7. $\begin{array}{r} 26 \\ \times 18 \\ \hline \end{array}$

8. $\begin{array}{r} 32 \\ \times 24 \\ \hline \end{array}$

9. $\begin{array}{r} \$74 \\ \times 16 \\ \hline \end{array}$

10. $\begin{array}{r} 69 \\ \times 36 \\ \hline \end{array}$

11. $\begin{array}{r} \$39 \\ \times 35 \\ \hline \end{array}$

12. $\begin{array}{r} 76 \\ \times 11 \\ \hline \end{array}$

13. $14 \times 53 =$ ______________

14. $\$26 \times 77 =$ ______________

15. $\$26 \times 74 =$ ______________

16. $21 \times 79 =$ ______________

### Mixed Review

Write the missing product.

17. $30 \times 19 = 570$, so $30 \times 18 = \square$

18. $65 \times 15 = 975$, so $65 \times 16 = \square$

19. $40 \times 21 = 840$, so $40 \times 22 = \square$

20. $\begin{array}{r} 29 \\ \times \ 5 \\ \hline \end{array}$

21. $\begin{array}{r} 17 \\ \times \ 4 \\ \hline \end{array}$

22. $\begin{array}{r} 38 \\ \times \ 9 \\ \hline \end{array}$

23. $\begin{array}{r} 52 \\ \times \ 8 \\ \hline \end{array}$

24. $\begin{array}{r} 91 \\ \times \ 3 \\ \hline \end{array}$

25. $12 \times 4 =$ ______________

26. $8 \times 8 =$ ______________

Name ______________________

# More About Multiplying by 2-Digit Numbers

Find the product. Estimate to check.

1. $\begin{array}{r} 221 \\ \times\ 17 \\ \hline \end{array}$

2. $\begin{array}{r} \$447 \\ \times\ 36 \\ \hline \end{array}$

3. $\begin{array}{r} 727 \\ \times\ 32 \\ \hline \end{array}$

4. $\begin{array}{r} 362 \\ \times\ 27 \\ \hline \end{array}$

5. $\begin{array}{r} 549 \\ \times\ 22 \\ \hline \end{array}$

6. $\begin{array}{r} \$7.29 \\ \times\ 46 \\ \hline \end{array}$

7. $\begin{array}{r} 636 \\ \times\ 34 \\ \hline \end{array}$

8. $\begin{array}{r} 659 \\ \times\ 73 \\ \hline \end{array}$

9. $74 \times 138 =$ ______

10. $25 \times 808 =$ ______

11. $89 \times \$465 =$ ______

12. $19 \times \$517 =$ ______

Find the value for *n* that makes the equation true.

13. $n \times 720 = 10{,}800$ ______

14. $491 \times n = 8{,}838$ ______

15. $n \times 679 = 5{,}432$ ______

**Mixed Review**

16. $(25 \div 5) + 10$ ______

17. $40 \div (2 \times 4)$ ______

18. $(48 \div 8) \times (3 + 8)$ ______

19. $(36 \div 4) + (12 \times 5)$ ______

20. $(15 \times 3) - (56 \div 8)$ ______

21. $(19 + 44) \div 7$ ______

22. $\begin{array}{r} 6{,}442 \\ +\ 2{,}192 \\ \hline \end{array}$

23. $\begin{array}{r} 4{,}612 \\ -\ 895 \\ \hline \end{array}$

24. $\begin{array}{r} 3{,}292 \\ -\ 2{,}890 \\ \hline \end{array}$

25. $\begin{array}{r} 6{,}505 \\ -\ 398 \\ \hline \end{array}$

26. $\begin{array}{r} 70 \\ \times\ 5 \\ \hline \end{array}$

27. $\begin{array}{r} 25 \\ \times\ 6 \\ \hline \end{array}$

28. $\begin{array}{r} 35 \\ \times\ 8 \\ \hline \end{array}$

29. $\begin{array}{r} 40 \\ \times\ 5 \\ \hline \end{array}$

30. $\begin{array}{r} 15 \\ \times\ 7 \\ \hline \end{array}$

Name ______________________________



# Choose a Method

Find the product. Estimate to check.

1. $\begin{array}{r} 2{,}001 \\ \times \quad 96 \\ \hline \end{array}$

2. $\begin{array}{r} \$2{,}425 \\ \times \quad 24 \\ \hline \end{array}$

3. $\begin{array}{r} 3{,}478 \\ \times \quad 47 \\ \hline \end{array}$

4. $\begin{array}{r} \$5{,}699 \\ \times \quad 26 \\ \hline \end{array}$

5. $\begin{array}{r} 1{,}527 \\ \times \quad 76 \\ \hline \end{array}$

6. $\begin{array}{r} 3{,}639 \\ \times \quad 69 \\ \hline \end{array}$

7. $\begin{array}{r} 7{,}498 \\ \times \quad 55 \\ \hline \end{array}$

8. $\begin{array}{r} 6{,}643 \\ \times \quad 78 \\ \hline \end{array}$

9. $48 \times 2{,}769 =$ ____________

10. $36 \times 4{,}873 =$ ____________

Exercises 11–12 show 2 common errors. Describe each error and correct it.

11. $\begin{array}{r} 1{,}360 \\ \times \ 42 \\ \hline 272 \\ 5{,}440 \\ \hline 5{,}712 \end{array}$

________________________________

________________________________

12. $\begin{array}{r} 2{,}966 \\ \times \quad 16 \\ \hline 17{,}796 \\ 29{,}660 \\ \hline 36{,}356 \end{array}$

________________________________

________________________________

## Mixed Review

13. $(4 \times 7) \times 5$ ____________

14. $(6 \times 10) \times 2$ ____________

15. $(40 \div 8) \times 12$ ____________

16. $\begin{array}{r} 19 \\ \times \ 60 \\ \hline \end{array}$

17. $\begin{array}{r} 29 \\ \times \ 11 \\ \hline \end{array}$

18. $\begin{array}{r} 32 \\ \times \ 28 \\ \hline \end{array}$

19. $\begin{array}{r} 2{,}511 \\ \times \ 16 \\ \hline \end{array}$

20. $\begin{array}{r} 787 \\ -\ 319 \\ \hline \end{array}$

21. $\begin{array}{r} 4{,}612 \\ -\quad 895 \\ \hline \end{array}$

22. $\begin{array}{r} 3{,}292 \\ -\ 2{,}890 \\ \hline \end{array}$

23. $\begin{array}{r} 6{,}908 \\ -\ 5{,}002 \\ \hline \end{array}$

Name ______________________



# Practice Multiplication

Find the product. Estimate to check.

1. 2,091 × 26
2. $5.84 × 6
3. 518 × 27
4. $3.20 × 84
5. 3,493 × 36
6. $45.39 × 31
7. 2,949 × 26
8. 813 × 63
9. $40.30 × 64
10. $5,403 × 38
11. 942 × 81
12. 3,009 × 49

## Mixed Review

13. School ended at 3:20 P.M. Ida walked to Sam's house, which took 20 minutes. She stayed there for 1 hour. Then she had to walk home. The walk from Sam's house to her home took 40 minutes. At what time did she get home?

14. Marilu's dad has some weights in the basement. Marilu is trying to lift a box with three 5-lb weights, seven 1-lb weights, and two 7-lb weights. How much weight is in the box?

Complete the table.

15.

| × | 5 | 7 | 2 | 8 | 3 | 9 | 12 | 6 |
|---|---|---|---|---|---|---|---|---|
| 12 | | | | | | | | |

16. 10,000 − 5,794
17. 25,000 − 21,211
18. 19,000 − 9,655
19. 31,000 − 28,414

Name ______________________



# Problem Solving Skill

## Multistep Problems

For 1–4, use the table.

The school cafeteria can add two new meals to the menu. They have been testing four meals and will choose the one that is most popular and the one that made the most money. The table shows the number of students who ate each meal and the price of the meal.

| Food | Number of Students | Price of Each Meal |
|---|---|---|
| chicken patties | 302 | \$1.12 |
| veggie burger | 309 | \$0.89 |
| cheese sandwich | 307 | \$0.95 |
| tomato soup | 189 | \$1.05 |

1. Write an expression to find the amount of money brought in by veggie burgers.

   ______________________

2. How much money is brought in by sales of tomato soup?

   ______________________

3. How much more money is brought in by chicken patties than by cheese sandwiches?

   ______________________

4. Which two new meals will the cafeteria staff choose?

   ______________________

   ______________________

## Mixed Review

5. \$12.27 × 3

6. \$8.99 × 4

7. \$11.15 − 7.27

8. \$19.89 − 6.40

9. $65 \times (437 - 81) = n$

   ______________________

10. $312 \times n = 24{,}336$

    ______________________

Name ______________________________



# Divide with Remainders

## Vocabulary

1. In a division problem, the ______________________ is the amount left over when a number cannot be divided evenly.

---

Make a model, record, and solve.

2. $4\overline{)19}$

3. $3\overline{)25}$

4. $6\overline{)38}$

5. $2\overline{)17}$

Divide. You may wish to use counters.

6. $7\overline{)61}$

7. $5\overline{)47}$

8. $3\overline{)19}$

9. $8\overline{)43}$

10. $6\overline{)58}$

11. $9\overline{)49}$

12. $2\overline{)13}$

13. $7\overline{)65}$

## Mixed Review

Complete each table.

| × | 4 | 5 | 9 | 3 | 11 | 7 | 6 | 10 |
|---|---|---|---|---|---|---|---|---|
| 6 | | | | | | | | |

| × | 11 | 12 | 5 | 8 | 7 | 4 | 6 | 2 |
|---|---|---|---|---|---|---|---|---|
| 12 | | | | | | | | |

Name ____________________



# Model Division

Make or draw a model. Record and solve.

1. 52 ÷ 3 = ____
2. 68 ÷ 4 = ____
3. 65 ÷ 5 = ____
4. 7)91
5. 6)100
6. 2)58
7. 63 ÷ 3 = ____
8. 78 ÷ 4 = ____
9. 53 ÷ 4 = ____
10. 2)38
11. 3)48
12. 6)72

## Mixed Review

For 13–15, use the table. The students in Mr. Jackson's class are holding a bake sale.

| Kind of Cookie | Total Number |
|---|---|
| Chocolate chip | 42 |
| Oatmeal | 65 |
| Ginger | 48 |

13. If Sara divides the chocolate chip cookies evenly into 3 bags, how many cookies does she put into each bag?

____________________

14. If Tim divides the oatmeal cookies evenly into 5 bags, how many cookies does he put into each bag?

____________________

15. Mr. Brown bought one bag of cookies for $1.75. What change should he receive from $10.00?

____________________

Find the sum or difference.

16. $17.50 + $17.50

17. $248.32 − $119.55

18. $49.68 − $5.11

19. $22.99 + $85.98

Name ______________________________



# Division Procedures

Divide and check.

1. $2\overline{)64}$ Check:

2. $3\overline{)96}$ Check:

3. $4\overline{)51}$ Check:

4. $3\overline{)94}$ Check:

5. $7\overline{)93}$ Check:

6. $8\overline{)89}$ Check:

## Mixed Review

7. Shari sold 114 boxes of cookies with 14 cookies in each box. How many cookies did she sell?

______________________________

8. A football stadium can seat 50,013 people. If 24,394 seats are empty, how many people are attending the game?

______________________________

9. $8 \times 9 = 72$

$9 \times 8 =$ ______

$72 \div$ ______ $= 8$

______ $\div 8 = 9$

10. $12 \times 7 =$ ______

$7 \times 12 =$ ______

$84 \div 7 =$ ______

$84 \div 12 =$ ______

11. $7 \times 6 =$ ______

______ $\times 7 = 42$

$42 \div 7 =$ ______

______ $\div 6 =$ ______

Name ______________________________ **LESSON 13.4**

# Problem Solving Strategy

## Predict and Test

Predict and test to solve.

1. There were 93 students going to a nature camp. After equal groups of fewer than 10 students, were formed for hiking, 2 students were left over. How many equal groups were formed?

   ______________________

2. During a hike, Sally and Dave collected 160 acorns. Sally collected 3 times as many acorns as Dave. How many acorns did Dave collect?

   ______________________

3. The 93 nature camp students ate lunch at the lodge. They sat at an even number of tables. There were 5 students sitting at one table, and an equal number of students sitting at each of the other tables. How many students were sitting at each of the other tables?

   ______________________

4. At one table, some of the students shared 3 pizzas. Each pizza was cut into 8 slices. After the students shared the pizza equally, there were 3 slices left over. How many students shared the pizza? How many slices of pizza did each student eat?

   ______________________

   ______________________

## Mixed Review

For 5–8, use the graph.

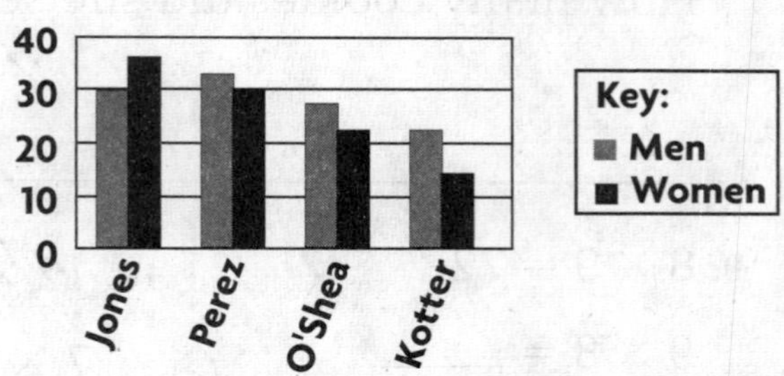


5. For which candidate is the difference between the number of men's and women's votes the greatest?

   ______________________

6. About how many women voted for Jones?

   ______________________

7. About how many men voted for O'Shea?

   ______________________

8. About how many people voted at Polling Station #3? ______________________

Name ____________________



# Mental Math: Division Patterns

Use a basic division fact and patterns to write each quotient.

1. $240 \div 6 =$ ______
   $2{,}400 \div 6 =$ ______
   $24{,}000 \div 6 =$ ______

2. $350 \div 5 =$ ______
   $3{,}500 \div 5 =$ ______
   $35{,}000 \div 5 =$ ______

3. $360 \div 4 =$ ______
   $3{,}600 \div 4 =$ ______
   $36{,}000 \div 4 =$ ______

Divide mentally. Write the basic division fact and the quotient.

4. $210 \div 3$ ______
5. $2{,}700 \div 3$ ______
6. $8{,}000 \div 2$ ______
7. $450 \div 9$ ______
8. $40{,}000 \div 8$ ______
9. $3{,}200 \div 8$ ______
10. $120 \div 4$ ______
11. $36{,}000 \div 6$ ______

## Mixed Review

For Problems 12–14, use the table at the right.

| ROAD MILEAGE FROM BOSTON, MA | |
|---|---|
| City | Number of Miles |
| Kansas City, MO | 1,391 |
| Philadelphia, PA | 296 |
| Houston, TX | 1,804 |

12. The Shaw family drove from Boston to Houston in 6 days. If they drove about the same distance each day, about how many miles did they drive each day?

______

13. The Peters family drove from Boston to Philadelphia in about 6 hours. About how many miles did they travel in one hour, if they traveled about the same distance each hour?

______

14. Tom and his family leave Boston on Monday morning to drive to Kansas City. If they drive about 200 miles each day, what day should they arrive in Kansas City?

______

Name ______________________



## Estimate Quotients

Choose the letter of the best estimate.

1. 359 ÷ 5    a. 70 or 80    b. 7 or 8    c. 15 or 20

2. 715 ÷ 7    a. 17 or 18    b. 10 or 11    c. 100 or 110

3. 156 ÷ 4    a. 12 or 13    b. 40 or 50    c. 4 or 5

Estimate by using compatible numbers.

4. 2)175    5. 4)231    6. 6)375    7. 8)255

8. 5)2,681    9. 4)3,289    10. 8)4,007    11. 3)1,811

12. 3)241    13. 5)4,787    14. 5)388    15. 7)3,594

**Mixed Review**

16. $2 \times 7 \times 2 =$ _____    17. $9 \times 5 \times 1 =$ _____    18. $2 \times 4 \times 7 =$ _____

19. $12 - 2 =$ _____ $+ 5$    20. $9 \times 9 =$ _____ $\div 2$

21. $20 +$ _____ $= 16 + 24$    22. $11 \times 6 =$ _____ $\div 3$

23. \$15.72 − \$ 8.03    24. 62,109 − 45,863    25. \$14.38 + \$57.60    26. 1,990 + 3,473

Name ______________________



# Problem Solving Skill

## Interpret the Remainder

Solve. Tell how you interpret the remainder.

1. The 158 fourth graders from the Glenwood School are going on a picnic. If there are 8 hot dogs in a package, how many packages are needed for each student to have 2 hot dogs?

______________________

______________________

2. Some of the students baked cookies for the picnic. Jeff baked 50 cookies. How many packages of 3 cookies each could he make?

______________________

______________________

3. The 158 students divide up into teams of 8 for a scavenger hunt. The students who are left over form a smaller team. How many teams are there?

______________________

______________________

4. Mrs. Jackson bought 7 dozen eggs for an egg-tossing contest. If each of 26 teams is given the same number of eggs, how many eggs are left over?

______________________

______________________

## Mixed Review

For 5–7, use the price list.

| SCHOOL STORE PRICE LIST | |
|---|---|
| **Item** | **Price** |
| Pencil | $0.10 |
| Eraser | $0.15 |
| Ruler | $0.50 |

5. Kito bought 4 pencils, 2 erasers, and a ruler. How much money did he spend?

______________________

6. On Monday, the store sold 20 pencils, 10 erasers, and 3 rulers. On Tuesday, the store sold 15 pencils, 13 erasers, and 3 rulers. On which day did the store take in more money?

______________________

7. On Friday, the store received a new supply of 72 pencils. Bill arranged the new pencils in groups of 5. How many groups could he make? How many pencils were left over?

______________________

Name ______________________________



# Find the Mean

## Vocabulary

Complete.

1. A(n) ______________ is the number found by dividing the sum of a set of numbers by the number of addends.

---

Write the division problem for finding the mean. Then find the mean.

2. 7, 7, 10, 12, 14 ______________

3. 3, 5, 6, 9, 12, 13 ______________

4. 143, 99, 213, 407, 698 ______________

5. 2,516; 6,518; 3,215; 4,327 ______________

Find the mean.

6. 2,178; 4,214; 1,291 ______________

7. 9,972; 2,755; 1,130 ______________

## Mixed Review

8. ______ × 1 = 7
______ × 10 = 70
______ × 100 = 700

9. ______ × 4 = 20
5 × ______ = 200
5 × ______ = 2,000

10. 8 × ______ = 56
______ × 70 = 560
8 × 700 = ______

11. 10 tens 5 ones = ______ tens 15 ones

12. 8 tens 17 ones = 9 tens ______ ones

13. 3 hundreds 14 tens = ______ hundreds 4 tens

14. 6 hundreds 2 tens = ______ hundreds 12 tens

Name ____________________

# Division Patterns to Estimate

Write the numbers you would use to estimate the quotient. Then estimate.

1. 58 ÷ 15 ____________
2. 695 ÷ 65 ____________
3. 556 ÷ 68 ____________
4. 273 ÷ 32 ____________
5. 447 ÷ 52 ____________
6. 810 ÷ 42 ____________

Estimate.

7. 45 ÷ 14 ____________
8. 362 ÷ 64 ____________
9. 596 ÷ 34 ____________
10. 79 ÷ 19 ____________
11. 462 ÷ 83 ____________
12. 721 ÷ 78 ____________

Complete the tables.

| | Dividend | Divisor | Quotient |
|---|---|---|---|
| 13. | 60 | ÷ 30 | ______ |
| 14. | ______ | ÷ 30 | 20 |
| 15. | 6,000 | ÷ 30 | ______ |
| 16. | ______ | ÷ 30 | 2,000 |

| | Dividend | Divisor | Quotient |
|---|---|---|---|
| 17. | 80 | ÷ 20 | ______ |
| 18. | ______ | ÷ 20 | 40 |
| 19. | ______ | ÷ 20 | 400 |
| 20. | 80,000 | ÷ 20 | ______ |

## Mixed Review

21. $\begin{array}{r} 39 \\ \times\ 67 \\ \hline \end{array}$

22. $\begin{array}{r} 379 \\ \times\ 46 \\ \hline \end{array}$

23. $\begin{array}{r} 3,593 \\ \times\ 4 \\ \hline \end{array}$

24. $\begin{array}{r} 5,201 \\ \times\ 82 \\ \hline \end{array}$

25. 81 ÷ 9 = ______
26. 140 ÷ 5 = ______
27. 320 ÷ 8 = ______
28. 72 ÷ 8 = ______
29. 660 ÷ 6 = ______
30. 490 ÷ 7 = ______

Name ______________________________



# Model Division

Make a model to divide.

1. $15\overline{)67}$

2. $28\overline{)118}$

3. $21\overline{)85}$

4. $32\overline{)100}$

5. $35\overline{)176}$

6. $37\overline{)115}$

7. $78 \div 25 =$ _____

8. $97 \div 13 =$ _____

9. $117 \div 22 =$ _____

Use the model to complete the number sentence.

10. 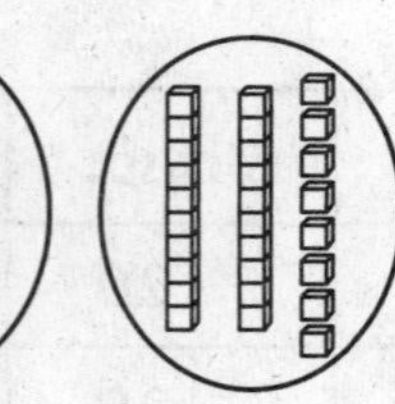

$61 \div 28 =$ _______

11. 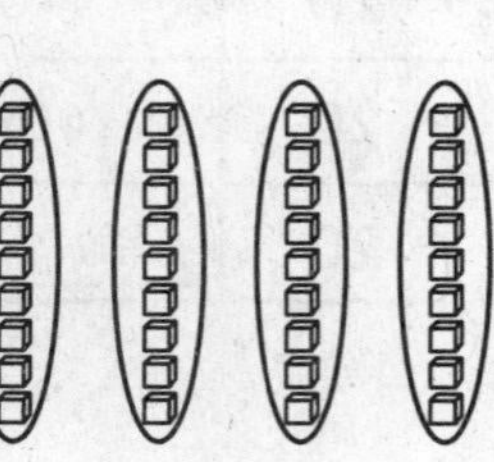

$38 \div 9 =$ _______

## Mixed Review

12. $100{,}000 \times 700$

13. $495 \times 39$

14. $\$872.64 - \$41.98$

15. $\$784.32 + \$32.53$

16. $200{,}000 \times 3{,}100$

17. $702 \times 44$

18. $\$90.89 - \$89.77$

19. $\$645.30 + \$822.98$

Name ____________________



## Division Procedures

Divide.

1. $22\overline{)598}$

2. $16\overline{)239}$

3. $11\overline{)346}$

4. $21\overline{)369}$

5. $13\overline{)461}$

6. $12\overline{)293}$

7. $31\overline{)862}$

8. $28\overline{)981}$

9. $17\overline{)206}$

10. $19\overline{)81}$

11. $23\overline{)485}$

12. $28\overline{)150}$

### Mixed Review

13. $4\overline{)532}$

14. $4\overline{)626}$

15. $7\overline{)921}$

16. $4\overline{)5,881}$

17. $90,008 - 66,849$

18. $967 \times 56$

19. $2,111 \times 16$

20. $72,931 + 30,275$

Name ______________________________



# Correcting Quotients

Write *too high, too low,* or *just right* for each estimate. Then divide.

1. $17\overline{)152}$ with estimate 8 ____________ ____________

2. $35\overline{)186}$ with estimate 4 ____________ ____________

3. $42\overline{)351}$ with estimate 7 ____________ ____________

4. $48\overline{)374}$ with estimate 8 ____________ ____________

5. $52\overline{)419}$ with estimate 7 ____________ ____________

6. $76\overline{)679}$ with estimate 8 ____________ ____________

7. $63\overline{)556}$ with estimate 9 ____________ ____________

8. $67\overline{)650}$ with estimate 9 ____________ ____________

## Mixed Review

9. Sue is packing 116 spools of thread into shoe boxes. Each box can hold 42 spools of thread. Will Sue be able to pack all the spools into 2 boxes? Explain.

____________________________

____________________________

10. Tony is estimating the time he needs to complete his math homework. He can complete about 3 problems per minute. If he allows 20 minutes, will he finish his 42 math problems? Explain.

____________________________

____________________________

Name ______________________________



# Problem Solving Skill

## Choose the Operation

Solve. Name the operation you used.

1. Mr. Murphy owns a bakery. On Saturday, he baked 60 blueberry muffins, 48 corn muffins, and 72 cranberry muffins. How many muffins did he bake in all?

______________________________

2. Mr. Murphy sold 498 cookies on Saturday. At the beginning of the day, there were 512 cookies. How many cookies were left at the end of the day?

______________________________

3. Susan bought 4 muffins for $0.79 each. How much money did she spend?

______________________________

4. Ryan paid $2.34 for 6 chocolate chip cookies. How much did each cookie cost?

______________________________

## Mixed Review

For 5–7, use the graph.

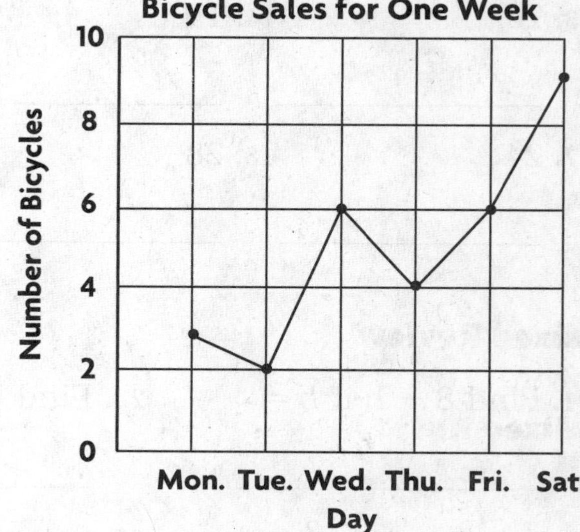


5. How many bicycles were sold on Wednesday?

______________________________

6. How many bicycles were sold during the week?

______________________________

7. How many more bicycles were sold on Saturday than on Monday?

______________________________

8. Will wants to buy a bicycle that costs $109. He has already saved $45. If Will earns $8 each week, how many weeks will it take him to save enough money to buy the bicycle?

______________________________

9. Some days, Mary rides her bicycle to and from school. The distance is 2 miles each way. In October, Mary rode her bicycle to and from school 14 times. How many miles did she ride to and from school in October?

______________________________

Name ______________________



## Factors and Multiples

List the factors you can find in a multiplication table for each product.

**1.** 16 **2.** 36 **3.** 81 **4.** 20

**5.** 48 **6.** 72 **7.** 32 **8.** 63

Use a multiplication table to find four multiples for each number.

**9.** 4 **10.** 9 **11.** 6 **12.** 3

Use what you know about multiplication. Find as many factors as you can for each product.

**13.** 20 **14.** 14 **15.** 6 **16.** 23

**17.** 24 **18.** 28 **19.** 19 **20.** 64

### Mixed Review

**21.** Find $8 - b$ if $b = 4$.

**22.** Find $80 \div m$ if $m = 8$.

**23.** Find $t \times 7$ if $t = 9$.

**24.** 4 weeks = __?__ days

**25.** $8 + n = 2 \times 9$

**26.** $6{,}511 \times 5$

**27.** $810 \div 90 =$

**28.** $367 \div 21 =$

**29.** $40 \times 600 =$

Name ______________________________



# Factor Numbers

Write an equation for the arrays shown.

1. 

2.

3. 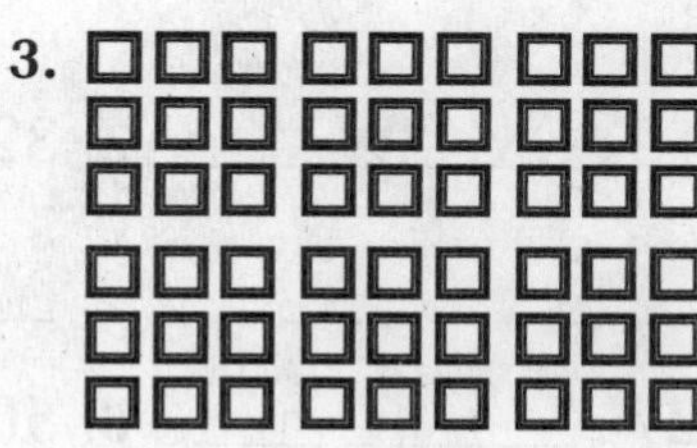

Write two ways to break apart the model.

4.

5. 

6.

Write at least two ways to break down the number.

7. 56 ______

8. 12 ______

9. 42 ______

10. 36 ______

11. 24 ______

12. 60 ______

## Mixed Review

13. $\begin{array}{r} 8{,}516 \\ 563 \\ +\ 518 \\ \hline \end{array}$

14. $\begin{array}{r} 648{,}518 \\ +\ 315{,}849 \\ \hline \end{array}$

15. $\begin{array}{r} 900{,}002 \\ +\ 95{,}518 \\ \hline \end{array}$

16. $789 \div 33$ ______

17. $462 \div 15$ ______

18. $929 \div 31$ ______

19. $5{,}017 \div 6$ ______

Name ______________________________



## Prime and Composite Numbers

Make arrays to find the factors. Write *prime* or *composite* for each number.

**1.** 19 ________ **2.** 32 ________ **3.** 81 ________ **4.** 36 ________

**5.** 27 ________ **6.** 56 ________ **7.** 29 ________ **8.** 18 ________

Write *prime* or *composite* for each number.

**9.** 42 **10.** 64 **11.** 100 **12.** 72

**13.** 22 **14.** 15 **15.** 91 **16.** 47

Frances has to put cans on a shelf. Each shelf must have an equal number of cans. How many ways can she put the cans on the shelf? List the ways.

**17.** 12 CANS

**18.** 24 CANS

**19.** 18 CANS

### Mixed Review

**20.** Train A traveled the 29 miles between Dell City and Mesabi 18 times. Train B traveled the 21 miles between Mesabi and Dodge 24 times. Which train traveled the greatest number of miles?

**21.** Joanna left school at 3:30 P.M. She went to volleyball practice for 90 minutes. She stopped at her aunt's house for 75 minutes, and then spent 15 minutes walking home. What time did she get home?

Name ____________________



# Find Prime Factors

Write each as a product of prime factors.

**1.** 36 ______ **2.** 81 ______ **3.** 18 ______ **4.** 27 ______

**5.** 34 ______ **6.** 55 ______ **7.** 38 ______ **8.** 40 ______

**9.** 32 ______ **10.** 56 ______ **11.** 72 ______

**12.** 88 ______ **13.** 20 ______ **14.** 144 ______

Write the missing factor.

**15.** $66 = 3 \times$ ■ ______

**16.** $98 = 2 \times$ ■ ______

**17.** $56 = 2 \times 2 \times 2 \times$ ■ ______

**18.** $100 = 2 \times 2 \times$ ■ $\times$ ■ ______

## Mixed Review

**19.** Order from *greatest* to *least:* 7,077; 7,707; 7,070; 7,700; 7,770; 7,777

______

______

**20.** Order from *least* to *greatest:* 4,106; 416; 4,601; 601; 4,001

______

______

**21.** Estimate. $9{,}083 \times 59$ ______

**22.** Estimate. $4,593 – $2,279 ______

**23.** Estimate. $6\overline{)55}$ ______

**24.** Estimate. $9\overline{)85}$ ______

Name ______________________________

# Problem Solving Strategy

## Find a Pattern

**1.** Continue the pattern.

1, 4, 7, 10, ___

______________________

**2.** Continue the pattern.

3, 9, 27, 81, ___

______________________

**3.** Describe the pattern in Exercise 1.

______________________

**4.** Describe the pattern in Exercise 2.

______________________

**5.** What are the next two numbers in the following sequence?

1, 3, 7, 13, 21, ___, ___

______________________

**6.** What are the next two shapes in the following sequence?

○□○□□○□□□○□□ ___ ___

______________________

**7.** Monica is playing a guessing game with her friends. When they say 5, she says 20. When they say 9, she says 36. When they say 2, she says 8. What is the pattern?

______________________

**8.** Ruthie is writing a pattern where she gets a number by multiplying the last number by 2 and adding 3. Write the next two numbers.

1, 5, 13, 29, ___, ___

______________________

## Mixed Review

**9.** Melanie's family took a trip. The first day they drove 140 miles. The second day they drove 210 miles. The third day they drove 120 miles. The last day they drove 190 miles. What was their average mileage per day?

______________________

**10.** Melanie's mother bought 30 gallons of gasoline during their trip. If they drove a total of 660 miles, how many miles did they drive per gallon of gasoline?

______________________

**11.** If gasoline cost $1.45 per gallon, how much did Melanie's mother spend on gasoline for their trip?

______________________

**12.** How much less would the total cost for gasoline have been if it had cost $1.25 per gallon?

______________________

Name ______________________________



# Lines, Rays, and Angles

## Vocabulary

Fill in the blanks.

1. A ray is part of a line and has one endpoint.
2. When two rays have the same endpoint, they form an ________.
3. A right angle angle forms a square corner.
4. An Acute angle is *less than* the measure of a right angle.
5. An obtuse angle is *greater than* the measure of a right angle.

Draw and label an example of each.

6. point *D*

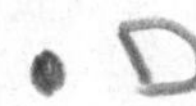


7. line *MN*

8. ray *DE*

What kind of angle is each? Write *right, acute,* or *obtuse.*

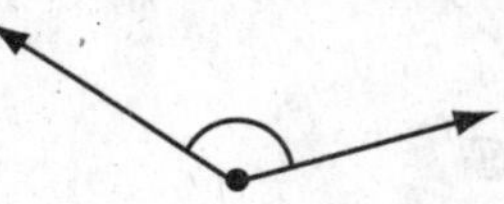

9. Obtuse

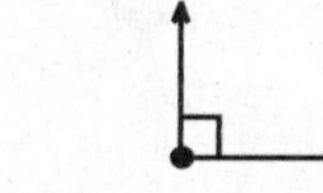

10. right

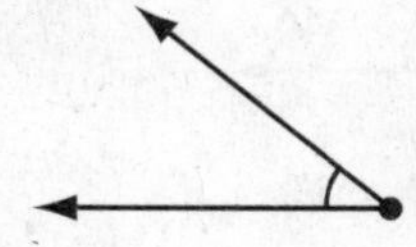

11. Acute

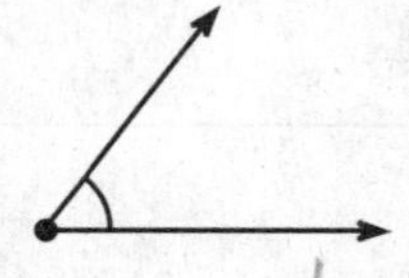

12. Acute

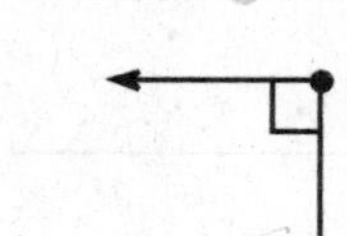

13. right

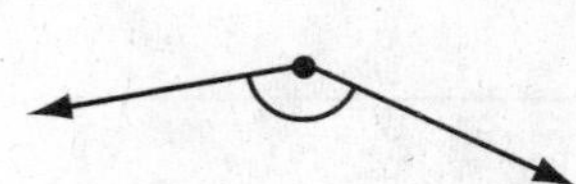

14. obtuse

## Mixed Review

15. $9 \times 7 =$

16. $8 \times 8 =$

17. $7 \times 4 = 28$

18. $10 \times 6 = 60$

19. $14 \div 2 =$ 7

20. $36 \div 6 =$ 6

21. $42 \div 6 =$ 7

Name ______________________________



# Line Relationships

## Vocabulary

Fill in the blanks.

1. ______________ lines are lines that cross each other.

2. ______________ lines intersect to form four right angles.

---

Name any line relationship you see in each figure. Write *intersecting, parallel,* or *perpendicular.*

3. 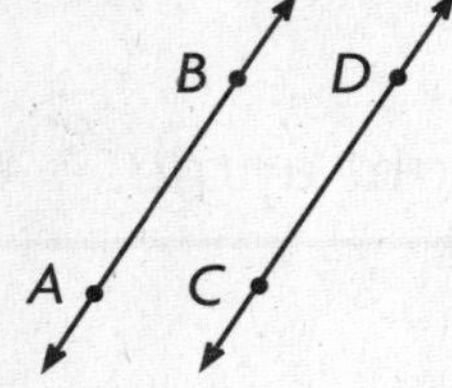


______________

______________

4. 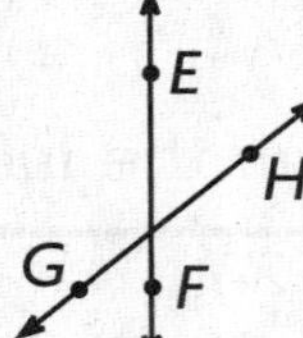


______________

______________

5. 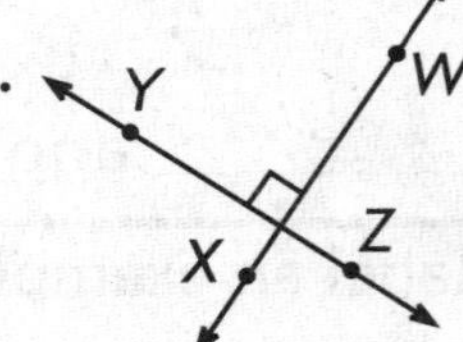


______________

______________

6. 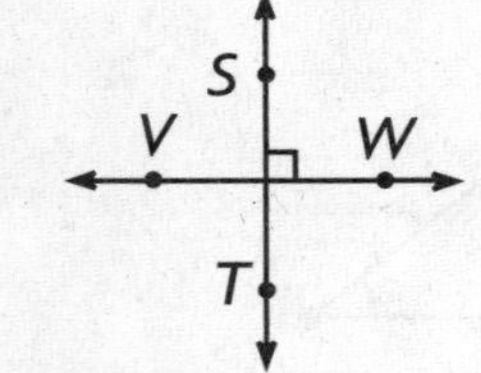


______________

______________

7. 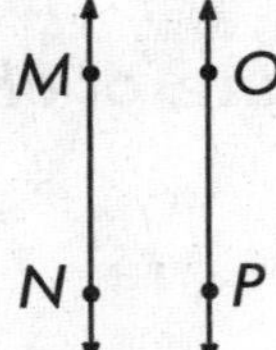


______________

______________

8. 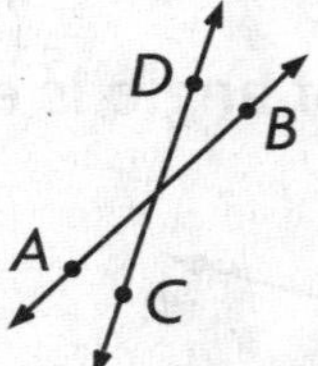


______________

______________

## Mixed Review

9. $4\overline{)22}$

10. $7\overline{)50}$

11. $9\overline{)14}$

12. $2\overline{)75}$

13. $\begin{array}{r} 17 \\ \times\ 15 \\ \hline \end{array}$

14. $\begin{array}{r} 259 \\ \times\ \ \ 5 \\ \hline \end{array}$

15. $\begin{array}{r} 78 \\ \times\ \ 9 \\ \hline \end{array}$

16. $\begin{array}{r} 361 \\ \times\ \ 20 \\ \hline \end{array}$

Name ______________________________



# Congruent Figures and Motion

Tell how each figure was moved. Write *slide, flip,* or *turn.*

1. 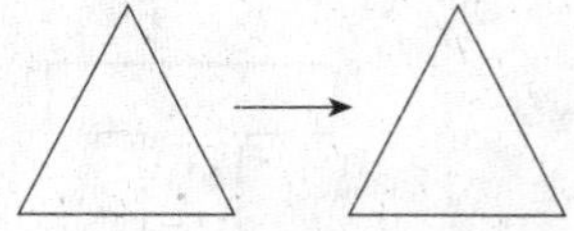
2. 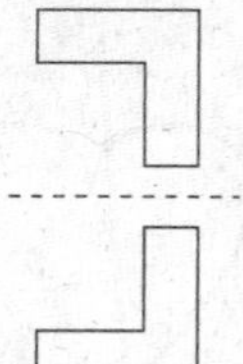
3. 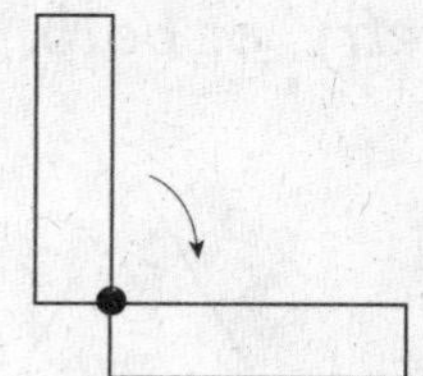

Tell whether the two figures are *congruent, similar,* or *neither.*

4. 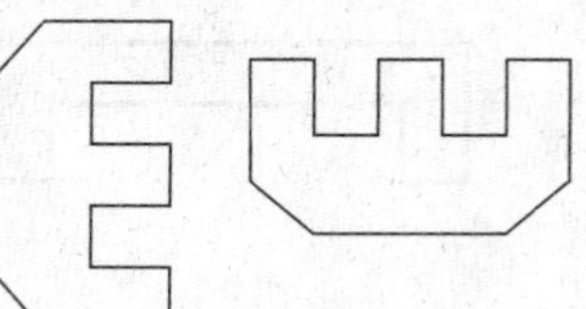
5. 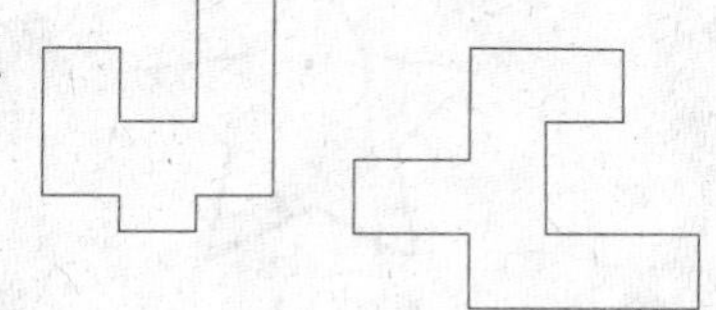
6. 

7. Copy this figure on dot paper. Then draw figures to show a slide, a flip, and a turn.

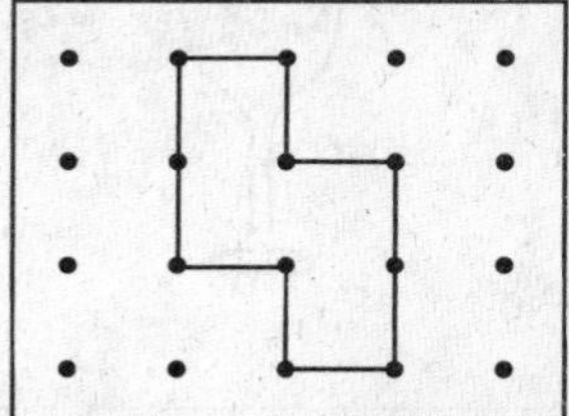

## Mixed Review

8. 4,729 − 2,418 = ________
9. 2,470 − 981 = ________
10. 1,897 + 423 = ________
11. 6,231 + 4,865 = ________
12. 10,078 − 9,021 = ________
13. 9,624 − 3,071 = ________

14. 738 + 389 + 388 + 296
15. 199 + 309 + 374 + 902
16. 422 + 688 + 201 + 114
17. 237 + 640 + 888 + 315

Name ________________________________



## Symmetric Figures

Tell whether the figure has *rotational symmetry, line symmetry,* or *both.*

**1.** 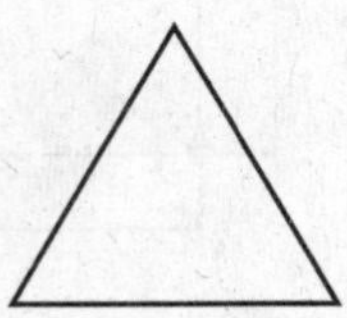

________________

**2.** 

________________

**3.** 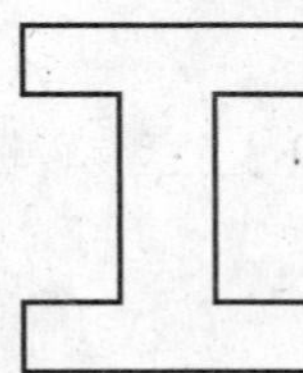

________________

**4.** 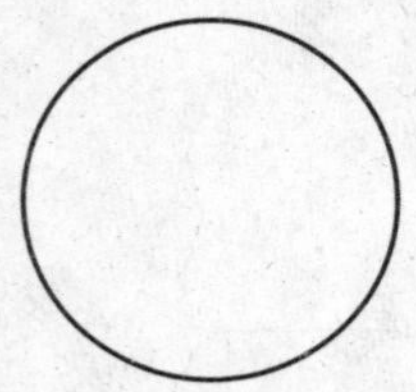

________________

**5.** 

________________

**6.** 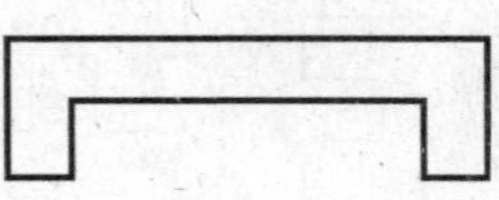

________________

**7.** 

________________

**8.** 

________________

**9.** 

________________

### Mixed Review

Write each number in expanded form.

**10.** 5,654 = ______ + ______ + ______ + ______

**11.** 9,232 = ______ + ______ + ______ + ______

**12.** 138,045 = ______ + ______ + ______ + ______ + ______

**13.** 87,657 = ______ + ______ + ______ + ______ + ______

Solve.

**14.** $(7 \times 6) \div 2 =$ ______ **15.** $(13 - 8) \times 9 =$ ______ **16.** $6 + (12 \div 2) =$ ______

**17.** $7{,}614 + 8{,}093$

**18.** $21{,}355 - 9{,}787$

**19.** $3{,}630 \times 41$

**20.** $2{,}498 \times 15$

Name ___



# Problem Solving Strategy

## Make a Model

For 1–4, make a model to solve.

1. Laura wants to make the figure below larger and then put it on her folder. Use 1-inch grid paper to help Laura make a larger picture.

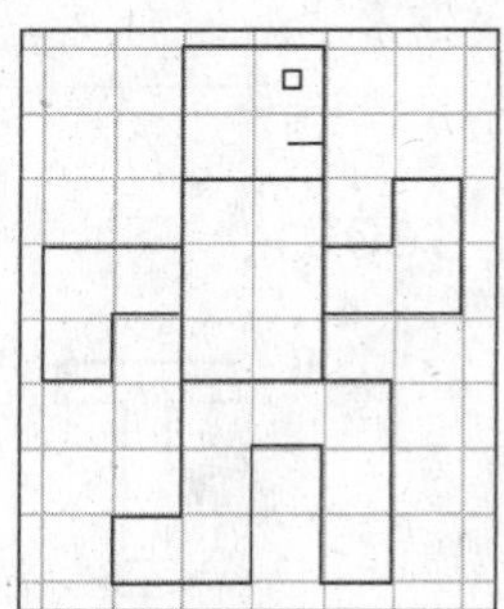

2. Wesley wants to decorate a bulletin board in his school hallway. He wants to make a larger picture of the figure below. Use 1-inch grid paper to help Wesley make the picture larger.

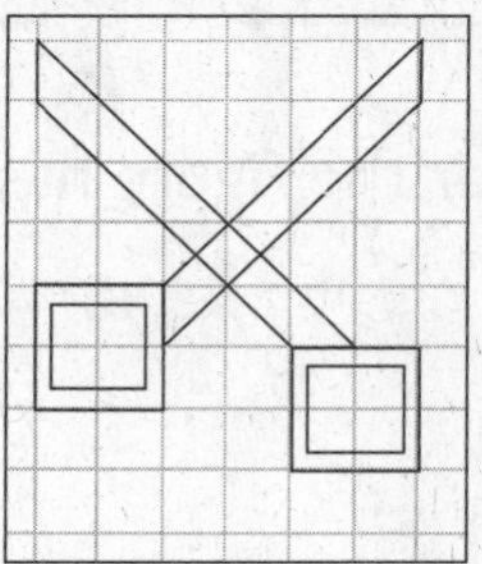

3. Make a smaller picture of the figure below. Use 0.5-cm grid paper to help you make a smaller picture.

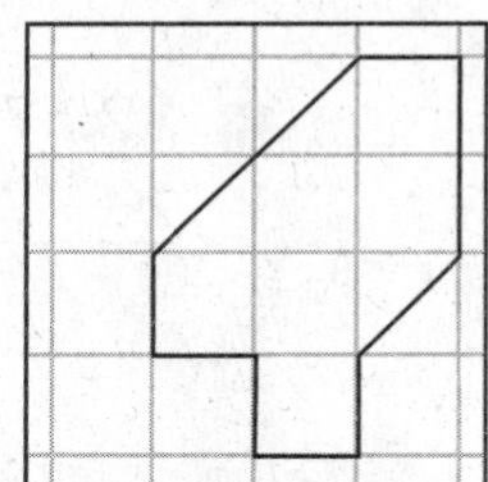

4. Make a larger picture of the figure below. Use 1-inch grid paper to help you.

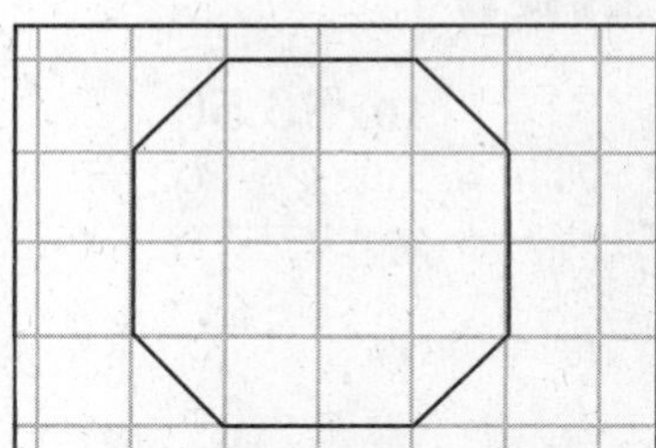

## Mixed Review

5. $589 + 782$

6. $5468 + 9230$

7. $10860 - 8701$

8. $1792 + 4567$

9. $907 - 488$

10. $800 + 745$

11. $3459 - 2899$

12. $6378 + 8719$

13. $6448 - 1714$

Name ______________________________ LESSON 18.1

# Turns and Degrees

Tell whether the rays on the circle show a $\frac{1}{4}$, $\frac{1}{2}$, $\frac{3}{4}$, or full turn.

1. 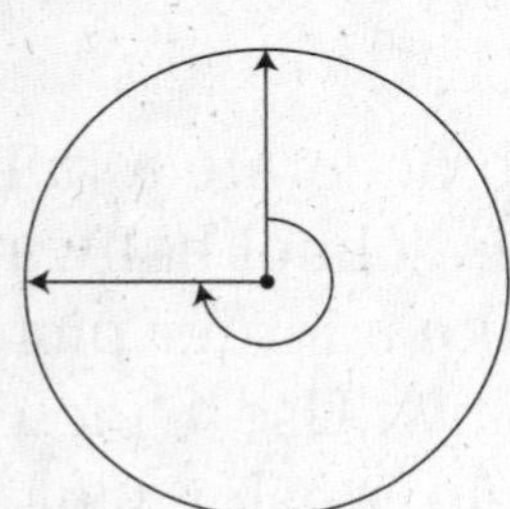
____________

2. 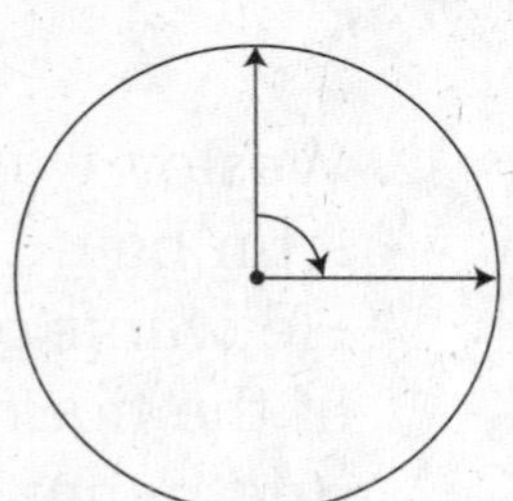
____________

3. 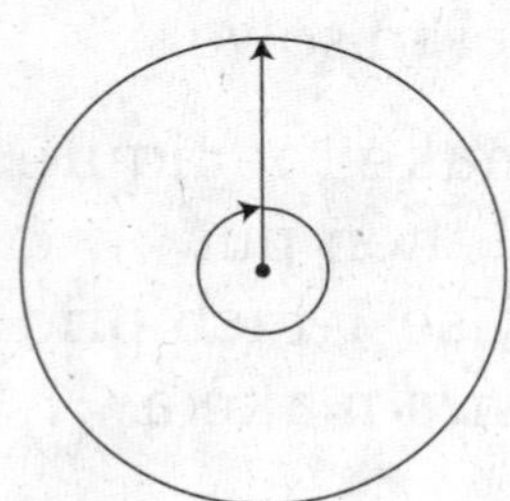
____________

4. 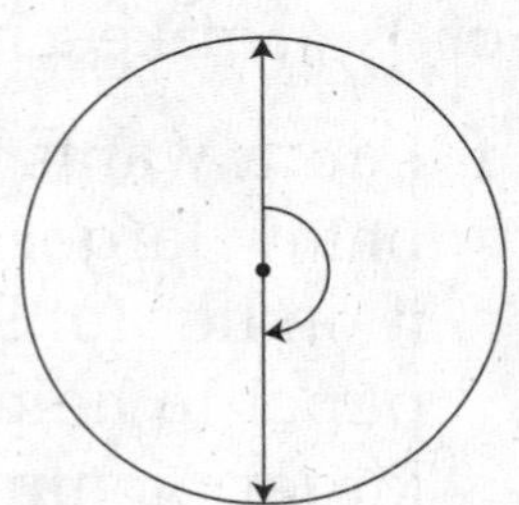
____________

Tell whether the figure has been turned 90°, 180°, 270°, or 360°.

5. 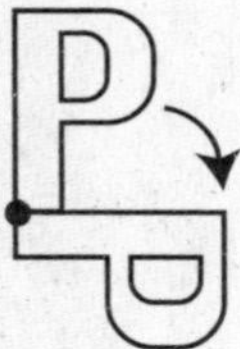

____________

6. 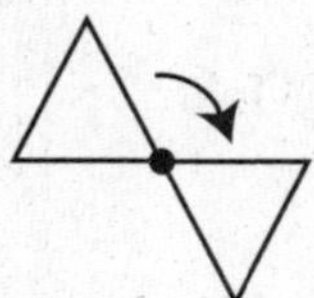
____________

7. 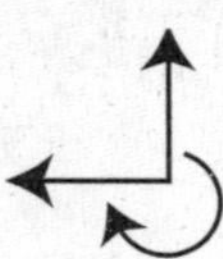
____________

8. 

____________

## Mixed Review

9. $\$2.35 \times 3$

10. $\$6.56 \times 9$

11. $\$1.87 \times 5$

12. $\$13 \times 12$

13. $\$2.57 \times 2$

14. $\$12.49 \times 3$

15. $\$9.15 \times 8$

16. $\$273 \times 22$

17. $\$196 \times 18$

18. $\$626 \times 6$

19. $\$3.78 \times 9$

20. $\$10.50 \times 9$

21. $\$689 \times 15$

22. $\$187 \times 13$

23. $\$345 \times 15$

Divide.

24. $19\overline{)86}$

25. $34\overline{)139}$

26. $25\overline{)406}$

Name ______________________________



# Measure Angles

Use a protractor to measure the angle.

1.

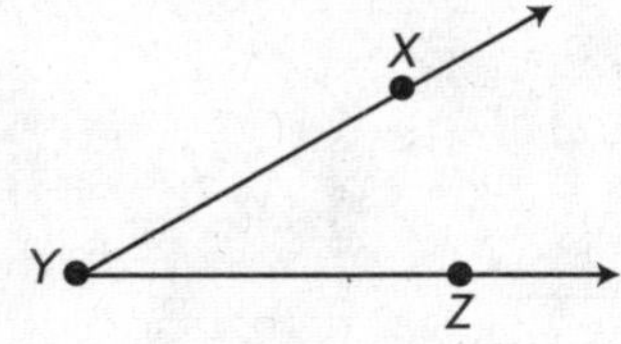


______

2.

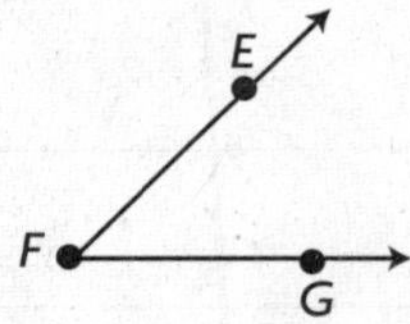


______

3.

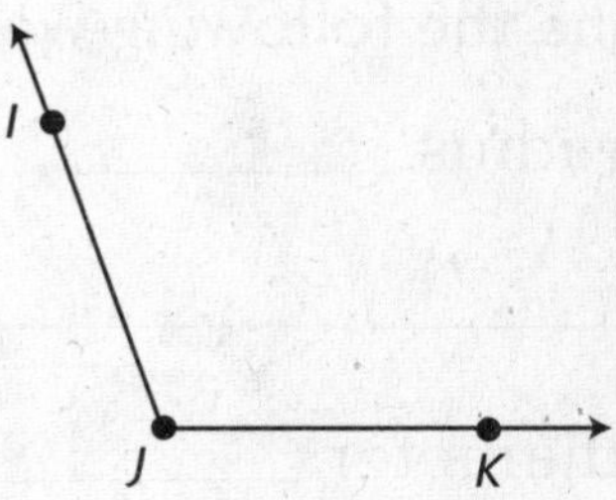


______

4.

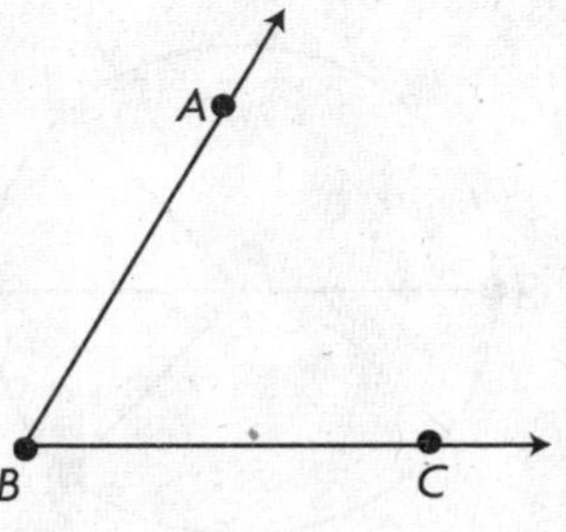


______

5.

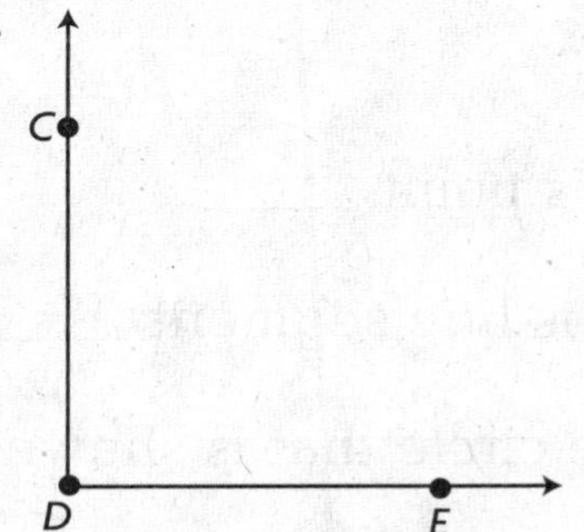


______

6.

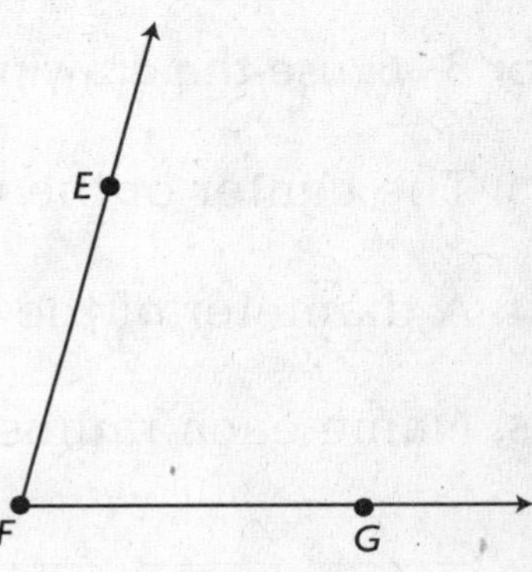


______

## Mixed Review

Name any line relationships you see in each figure.
Write *intersecting, parallel,* or *perpendicular lines.*

7.

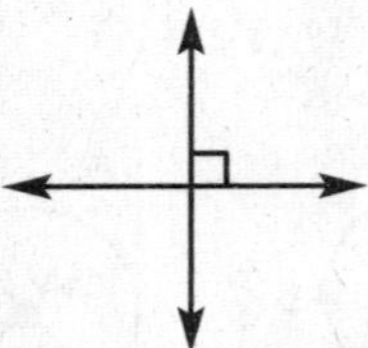

______

8.

______

9.

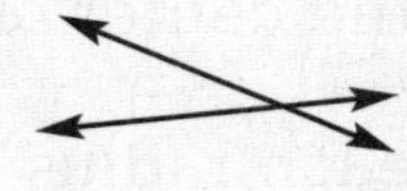

______

10.

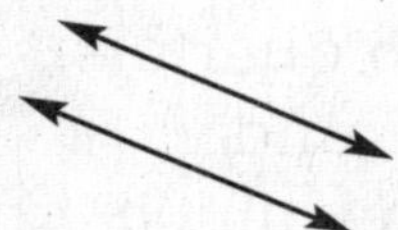

______

11.

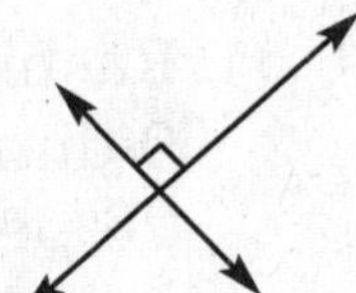

______

12.

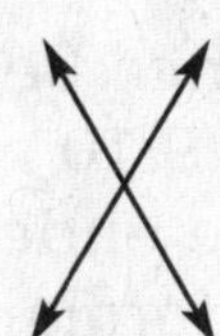

______

Name ______________________________

# Circles

## Vocabulary

Define the following words.

1. radius: ______________________________

______________________________

2. diameter: ______________________________

______________________________

---

For 3–6, use the drawing.

3. The center of the circle is point _____.

4. A diameter of the circle is line segment _____.

5. Name each radius of the circle that is shown.

_____, _____, _____, and _____

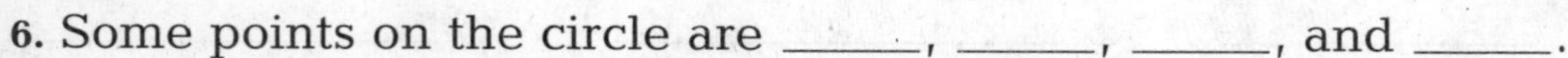

6. Some points on the circle are _____, _____, _____, and _____.

7. Draw a circle. Label the center point *A*. Draw a radius $\overline{AB}$. Draw a diameter $\overline{CD}$.

For 8–9, use Circles *R* and *W*.

8. Name the center of each circle. __________

9. Name each radius shown. ______________________________

______________________________

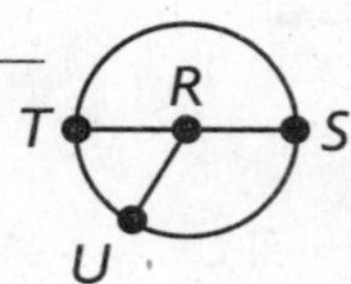


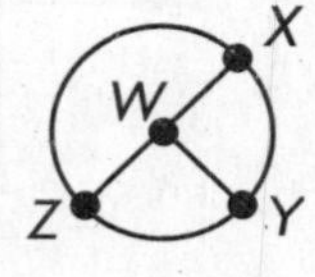


## Mixed Review

10. A performance began at 7:15 P.M. At 9:10 P.M., the performance ended. How long was the performance?

______________________________

11. Rashid's bank has 6 quarters, 9 dimes, 15 nickels, and 26 pennies in it. How much is in his bank?

______________________________

Name ______________________



# Circumference

Estimate each circumference.

1.

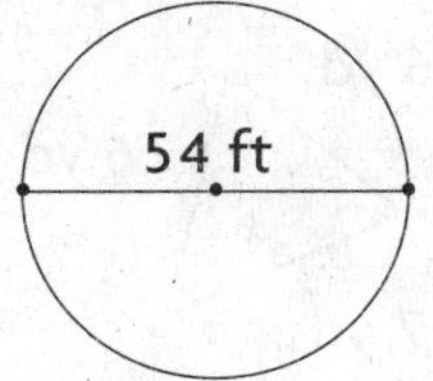


______________

2.

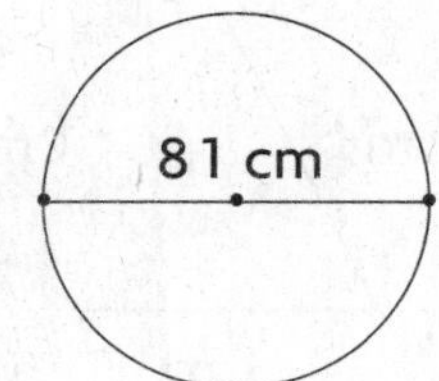


______________

3.

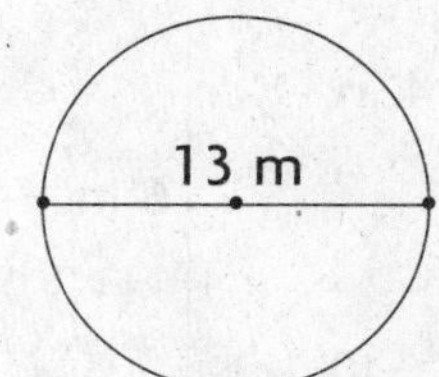


______________

4.

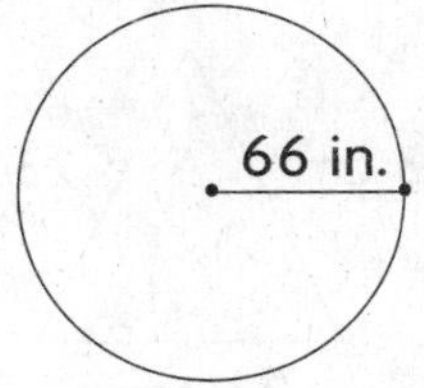


______________

5.

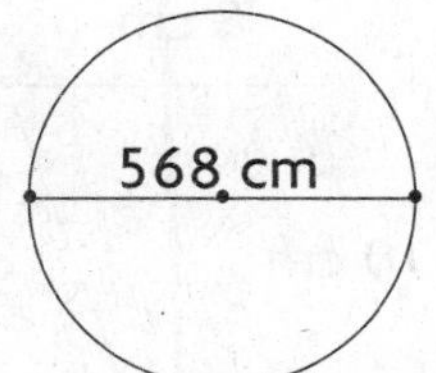


______________

6.

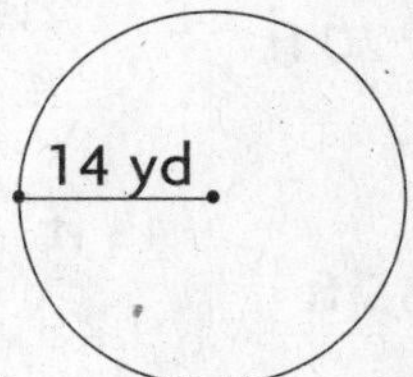


______________

7.

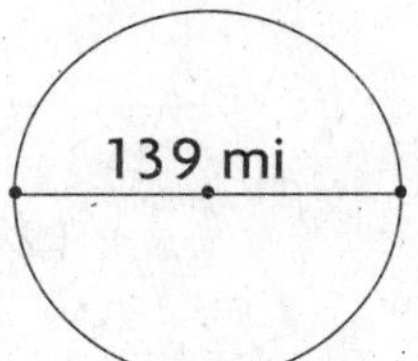


______________

8.

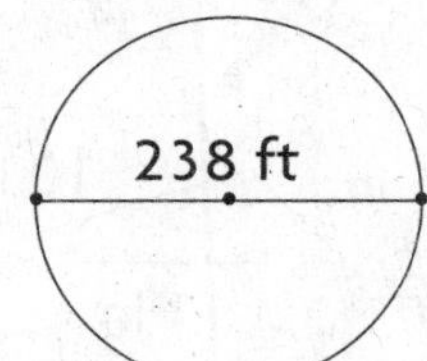


______________

9.

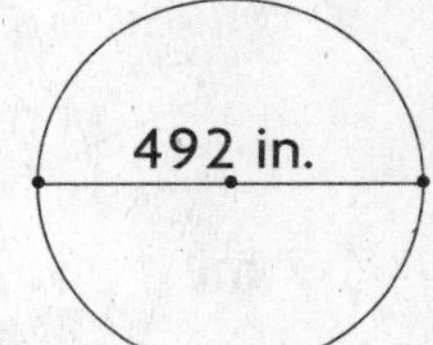


______________

10. A wheel has a circumference of 8 inches. It rolls 72 inches. How many complete turns did the wheel make?

______________

## Mixed Review

Write the number in word form.

11. 7,849 ______________

12. 182 ______________

13. 1,283 ______________

14. 9,634 ______________

15. 17,334 ______________

Name ______________________

LESSON 18.5

# Classify Triangles

Classify each triangle. Write *isosceles, scalene,* or *equilateral.*

1. 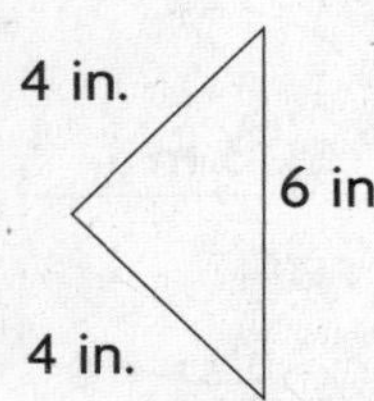


2. 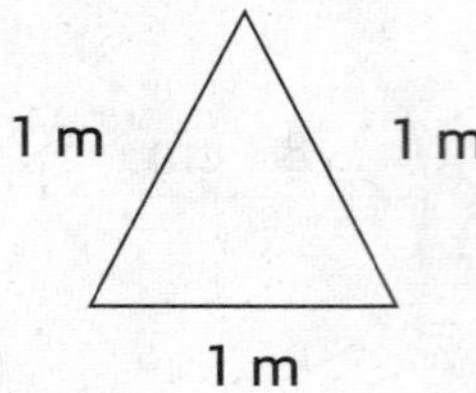


3. 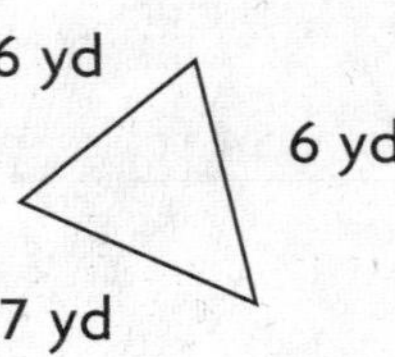


4. 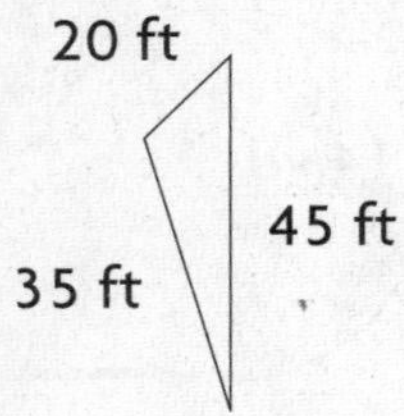


5. 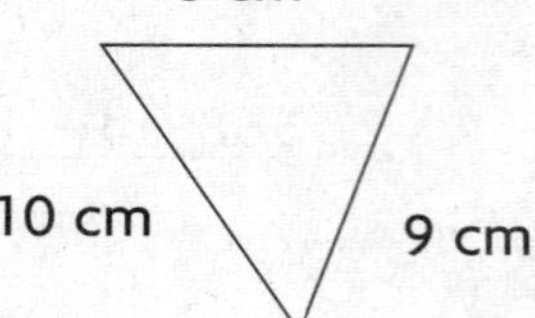


6. 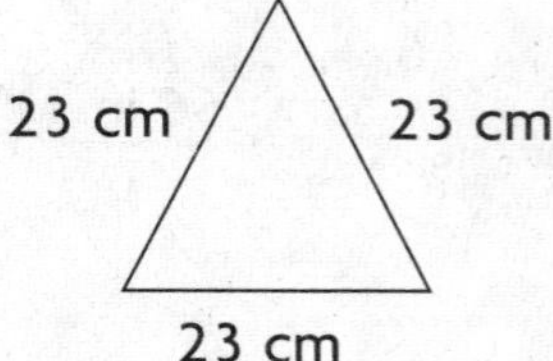


7. 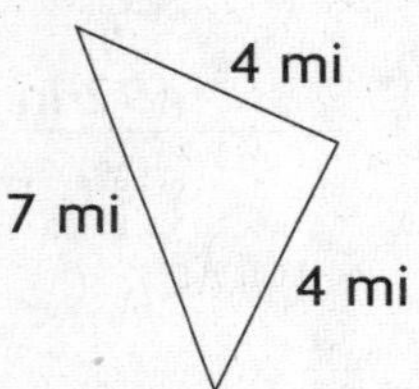


8. 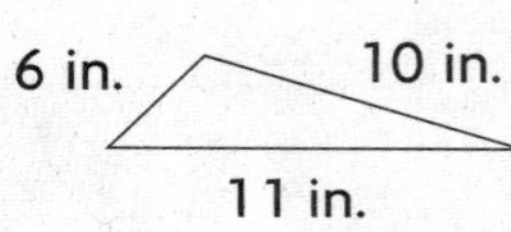


9. 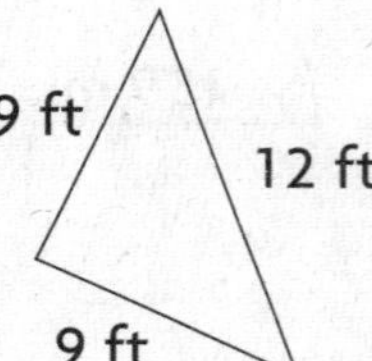


Classify each triangle by the length of its sides. Write *isosceles, scalene,* or *equilateral.*

10. 12 in., 12 in., 12 in.

11. 65 yd, 43 yd, 65 yd

12. 45 mi, 23 mi, 56 mi

## Mixed Review

Tell whether the figure has *rotational symmetry, line symmetry,* or *both.*

13. 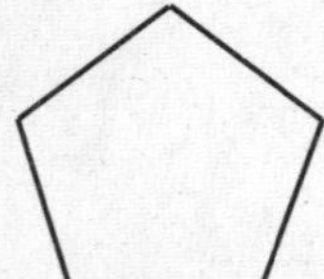

14. 

15. 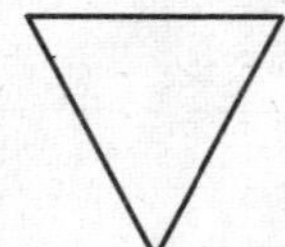

Name ______________________________



# Classify Quadrilaterals

## Vocabulary

Fill in the blanks.

**1.** All ______________ have 4 sides and 4 angles.

**2.** ______________ have only 2 sides that are parallel.

**3.** ______________ have 2 pairs of parallel sides. They have 2 acute angles of the same size and 2 obtuse angles of the same size.

**4.** A ______________ has 4 congruent sides. Its opposite sides are parallel and its angles may be right angles.

---

Classify each figure in as many ways as possible. Write *quadrilateral, parallelogram, square, rectangle, rhombus,* or *trapezoid.*

**5.** 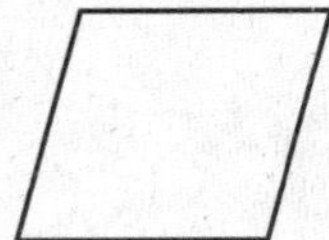

______________

______________

**6.** 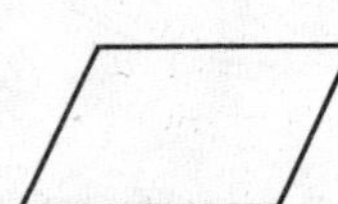

______________

______________

**7.** 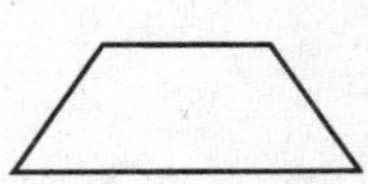

______________

______________

**8.** 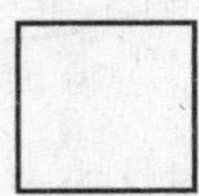

______________

______________

Draw an example of each quadrilateral.

**9.** trapezoid

**10.** square

**11.** rhombus

**12.** parallelogram

**13.** rectangle

**14.** general quadrilateral



## Mixed Review

**15.** $250 \times 7$

**16.** $864 \times 5$

**17.** $793 \times 6$

**18.** $122 \times 8$

Name ______________________________



# Problem Solving Strategy

## Draw a Diagram

Follow the directions.

1. Sort these figures into a Venn diagram showing *Figures with 4 Sides* and *Figures with More Than 4 Sides:* square, rectangle, pentagon, trapezoid, octagon, hexagon.

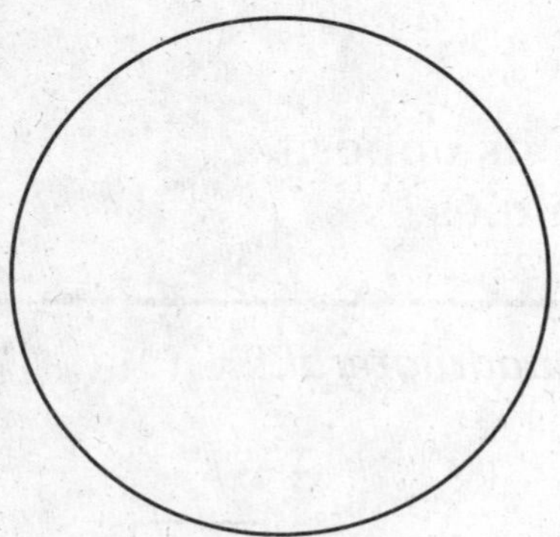

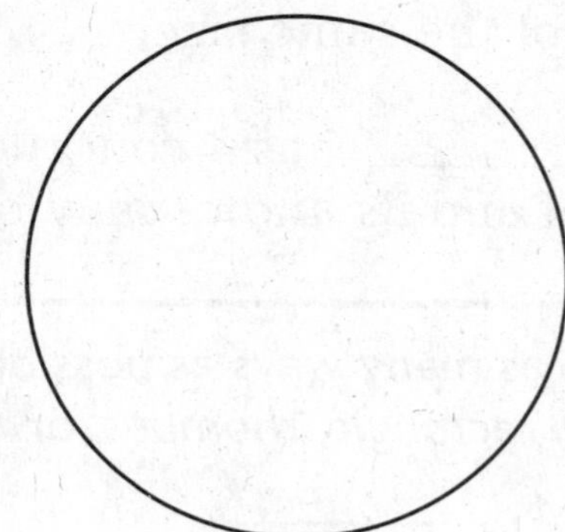

2. Sort these numbers into a Venn diagram showing *Divisible by 3* and *Not Divisible by 3:* 28, 35, 36, 40, 51, 60.

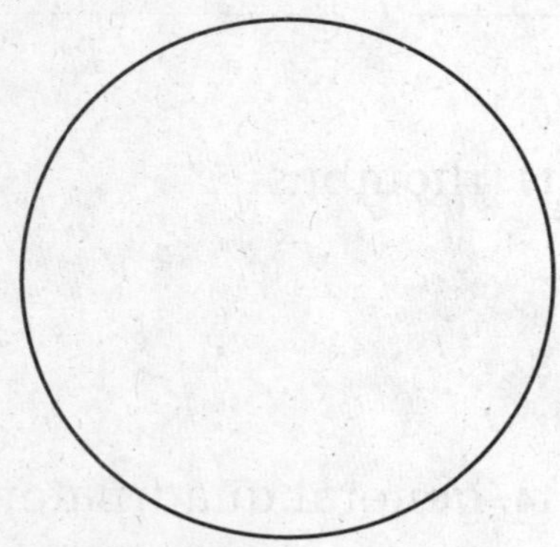

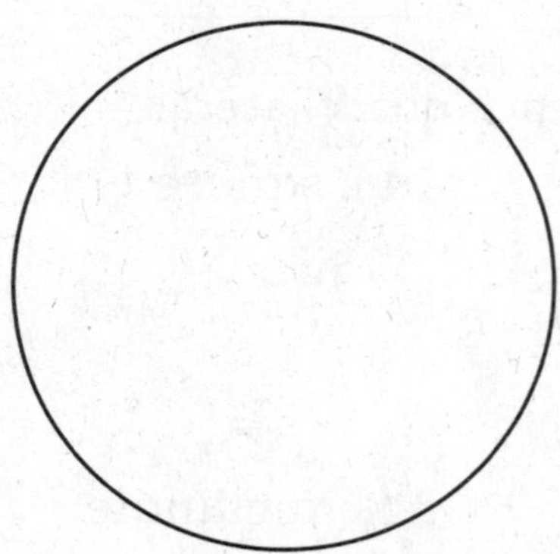

## Mixed Review

Add or subtract.

3. 6,783 + 3,960

4. 8,743 − 586

5. 54,732 + 4,694

6. 9,275 + 2,392

7. 14,821 − 4,812

Name ______________________________

# Read and Write Fractions

## Vocabulary

Fill in the blank.

1. A number that names a part of a whole is a ____________.

---

Write a fraction for the shaded part. Write a fraction for the unshaded part.

2. 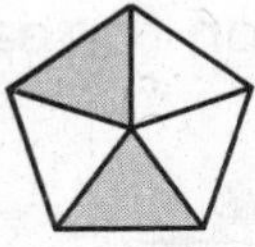
______

3. 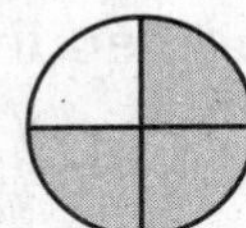
______

4. 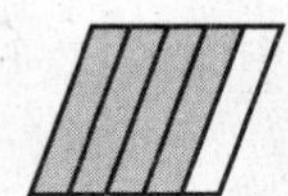
______

5. 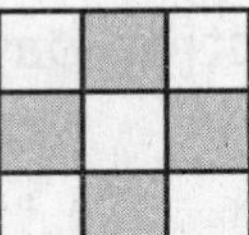
______

6. 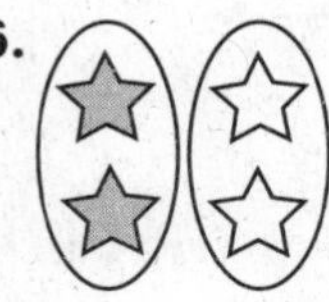
______

7. 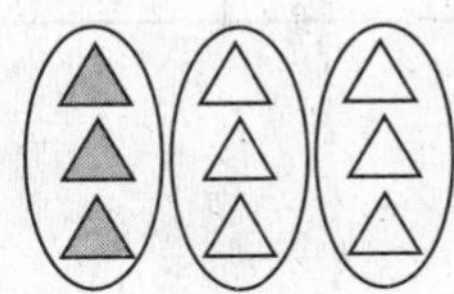
______

8. 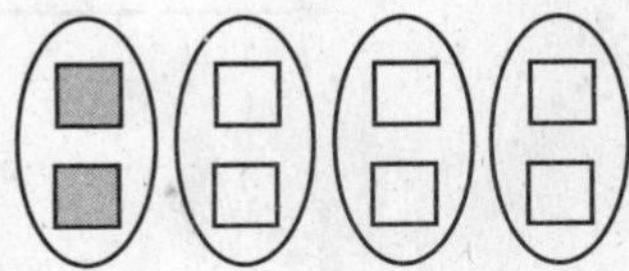
______

Draw a picture and shade part of it to show the fraction. Write a fraction for the unshaded part.

9. $\frac{2}{6}$
______

10. $\frac{7}{8}$
______

11. $\frac{4}{5}$
______

## Mixed Review

12. $12 \times 5$

13. $11 \times 7$

14. $9 \times 8$

15. $6 \times 6$

16. $12 \times 8$

17. $5\overline{)85}$

18. $9\overline{)81}$

19. $4\overline{)88}$

20. $12\overline{)144}$

21. $7\overline{)56}$

Name ______________________________

LESSON 19.2

# Equivalent Fractions

## Vocabulary

Fill in the blank.

1. Fractions that name the same amount are called ______________________________.

Use fraction bars or number lines to find at least one equivalent fraction for each.

2. $\frac{1}{4}$ = ________
3. $\frac{2}{3}$ = ________
4. $\frac{1}{2}$ = ________
5. $\frac{3}{6}$ = ________
6. $\frac{2}{8}$ = ________
7. $\frac{5}{6}$ = ________
8. $\frac{8}{12}$ = ________
9. $\frac{6}{8}$ = ________
10. $\frac{6}{12}$ = ________
11. $\frac{4}{12}$ = ________
12. $\frac{4}{5}$ = ________
13. $\frac{2}{5}$ = ________

## Mixed Review

14. $13 - 7 =$ ____ $\times 3$
15. $20 \div$ ____ $= 14 - 12$
16. ____ $+ 49 = 81 - 15$
17. $4 \times 12 = 48 \div$ ____
18. $63 +$ ____ $= 71 + 19$
19. $55 \div$ ____ $= 29 - 24$
20. $3 \times 3 \times 3 \times$ ____ $= 54$
21. $4 \times$ ____ $\times 2 = 32$
22. $7 \times 2 \times$ ____ $= 14$

Name ______________________________

# Add Like Fractions

Find the sum.

1. $\frac{3}{6} + \frac{1}{6} =$ ____

2. $\frac{1}{8} + \frac{6}{8} =$ ____

3. $\frac{3}{5} + \frac{4}{5} =$ ____

4. $\frac{5}{12} + \frac{2}{12} =$ ____

5. $\frac{6}{10} + \frac{7}{10} =$ ____

6. $\frac{3}{4} + \frac{2}{4} =$ ____

7. $\frac{2}{5} + \frac{1}{5}$

8. $\frac{5}{9} + \frac{4}{9}$

9. $\frac{2}{11} + \frac{4}{11}$

Compare. Write <, >, or = in each ○.

10. $\frac{2}{9} + \frac{3}{9}$ ○ $\frac{4}{9}$

11. $\frac{1}{6} + \frac{2}{6}$ ○ $\frac{1}{2}$

12. $\frac{5}{9} + \frac{8}{9}$ ○ 1

Find the value of *n*.

13. $\frac{2}{7} + \frac{4}{n} = \frac{6}{7}$ ________

14. $\frac{3}{13} + \frac{n}{13} = \frac{9}{13}$ ________

15. $\frac{6}{9} + \frac{1}{n} = \frac{7}{9}$ ________

16. $\frac{9}{n} + \frac{1}{4} = 1$ ________

## Mixed Review

17. 7 + 7 + 7 + 7 = ____

18. 12 + 12 + 12 + 12 + 12 = ____

19. $8 \times 7$

20. $10 \times 5$

21. $3 \times 9$

22. $7 \times 7$

23. $6 \times 9$

Write an equivalent fraction for each.

24. $\frac{7}{14} =$ ____

25. $\frac{16}{40} =$ ____

26. $\frac{12}{36} =$ ____

27. $\frac{9}{90} =$ ____

28. $\frac{6}{18} =$ ____

Name ______________________________



# Subtract Like Fractions

Use fraction bars to find the difference.

1. $\frac{3}{4} - \frac{2}{4} =$ ________ 2. $\frac{4}{6} - \frac{3}{6} =$ ________ 3. $\frac{7}{8} - \frac{3}{8} =$ ________

4. $\frac{5}{10} - \frac{3}{10} =$ ________ 5. $\frac{3}{5} - \frac{1}{5} =$ ________ 6. $\frac{6}{8} - \frac{2}{8} =$ ________

7. $\frac{10}{12} - \frac{5}{12} =$ ________ 8. $\frac{7}{10} - \frac{3}{10} =$ ________ 9. $\frac{5}{6} - \frac{1}{6} =$ ________

Find the difference.

10. 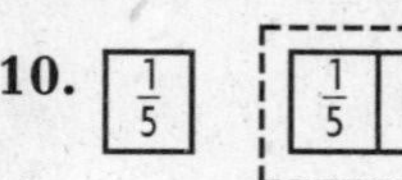


11. 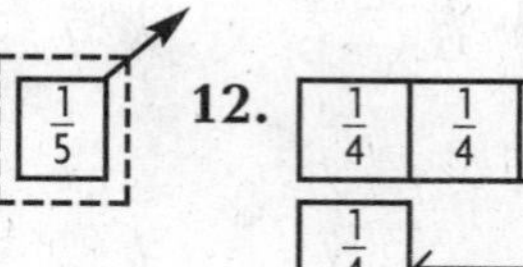


12. $\frac{1}{4}$ $\frac{1}{4}$ $\frac{1}{4}$ / $\frac{1}{4}$

13. $\frac{1}{4}$ $\frac{1}{4}$ / $\frac{1}{4}$

________ ________ ________ ________

Find the sum.

14. $\frac{1}{12} + \frac{5}{12} =$ ________ 15. $\frac{3}{8} + \frac{3}{8} =$ ________ 16. $\frac{4}{7} + \frac{5}{7} =$ ________

**Mixed Review**

17. $487 \times 22$ 18. $68 \times 95$ 19. $3,287 \times 17$ 20. $8,061 \times 40$

21. $15\overline{)30}$ 22. $5\overline{)30}$ 23. $3\overline{)30}$ 24. $4\overline{)36}$

Name ______________________

# Add and Subtract Mixed Numbers

Find the sum or difference.

1. $5\frac{7}{8} - 2\frac{3}{8}$

2. $6\frac{4}{10} + 4\frac{3}{10}$

3. $9\frac{3}{4} + 2\frac{2}{4}$

4. $3\frac{2}{3} - 2\frac{1}{3}$

5. $5\frac{4}{5} + 1\frac{2}{5}$

6. $8\frac{6}{8} - 3\frac{2}{8}$

7. $9\frac{8}{12} + 6\frac{4}{12}$

8. $4\frac{5}{6} - 3\frac{3}{6}$

9. $7\frac{8}{9} - 6\frac{1}{9}$

10. $9\frac{9}{10} + 5\frac{2}{10}$

11. $8\frac{2}{4} + 6\frac{1}{4}$

12. $3\frac{10}{12} - 1\frac{7}{12}$

13. $7\frac{4}{5} - 1\frac{3}{5} =$ ________

14. $9\frac{5}{8} + 4\frac{4}{8} =$ ________

15. $4\frac{6}{9} - 2\frac{2}{9} =$ ________

16. $5\frac{9}{12} + 2\frac{3}{12} =$ ________

17. $9\frac{2}{5} + 3\frac{1}{5} =$ ________

18. $6\frac{7}{10} - 2\frac{5}{10} =$ ________

Compare. Write <, >, or = in each ○.

19. $6\frac{1}{7} + 3\frac{5}{7}$ ○ 10

20. $3\frac{1}{4}$ ○ $1\frac{5}{8} + 1\frac{5}{8}$

21. $16\frac{7}{10} - 7\frac{7}{10}$ ○ 10

## Mixed Review

22. $48 + 78$

23. $63 - 57$

24. $140 - 79$

25. $224 + 865$

26. $370 - 263$

27. $586 - 139$

28. $428 + 765$

29. $831 - 156$

30. $605 - 384$

31. $372 - 189$

Name ______________________________

# Problem Solving Skill

## Choose the Operation

Write the operation. Then solve each problem.

1. Henry and Cyndi each ate $\frac{1}{3}$ of a small cake. What fraction of the cake did they eat?

______________________________

2. Linda baked a huge cookie for her friends. Sue ate $\frac{5}{8}$ of the cookie and Mary ate $\frac{3}{8}$. How much more of the cookie did Sue eat?

______________________________

3. Phillip likes to ride his bike, skateboard, and read in his spare time. He spends $\frac{2}{8}$ of his time riding his bike and $\frac{5}{8}$ of his time skateboarding. How much of his spare time does he have left to spend reading?

______________________________

4. Mr. Jones baked 12 cupcakes for the class party. Before lunch $\frac{3}{12}$ of the cupcakes were eaten. After lunch $\frac{5}{12}$ of the cupcakes were eaten. What fraction of the cupcakes were left for a snack after school?

______________________________

## Mixed Review

Solve.

5. At the end of five days Joseph had saved $30. If each day he saved $2 more than the day before, how much money did Joseph save each day?

______________________________

6. A series of numbers starts with 2. Each number in the series is two times as great as the number before it. What is the sixth number in the series?

______________________________

7. $20.22 + $15.24

8. $38.40 − $19.99

9. 2,649 − 1,670

10. 9,028 + 3,840

11. $38.20 + $88.79

Name ____________________



# Equivalent Decimals

## Vocabulary

Complete.

**1.** ____________________ are decimals that name the same number.

---

Are the two decimals equivalent? Write *yes* or *no*.

**2.** 0.4 and 0.40 ________

**3.** 0.1 and 0.01 ________

**4.** 0.50 and 0.5 ________

**5.** 0.20 and 0.02 ________

**6.** 0.3 and 0.30 ________

**7.** 0.80 and 0.8 ________

**8.** 0.9 and 0.90 ________

**9.** 0.18 and 0.81 ________

Write an equivalent decimal for each. You may use decimal models.

**10.** 0.7 ________

**11.** 0.1 ________

**12.** 0.60 ________

**13.** 0.4 ________

**14.** 0.20 ________

**15.** 0.8 ________

**16.** 0.30 ________

**17.** 0.5 ________

**18.** 0.90 ________

**19.** 0.3 ________

## Mixed Review

**20.** $\frac{7}{10} + \frac{7}{10} =$ ________

**21.** $1\frac{4}{5} + 1\frac{4}{5} =$ ________

**22.** $3\frac{8}{9} + 3\frac{8}{9} =$ ________

**23.** $5\frac{4}{5} - 1\frac{3}{5} =$ ________

**24.** $\frac{10}{9} + 3\frac{5}{9} =$ ________

**25.** $\frac{7}{6} - \frac{2}{3} =$ ________

**26.** $\frac{4}{7} + \frac{2}{7} =$ ________

**27.** $1\frac{3}{4} + 2\frac{3}{4} =$ ________

**28.** $7\frac{2}{3} + 6\frac{1}{3} =$ ________

**29.** $\frac{3}{4} - \frac{1}{2} =$ ________

**30.** $6\frac{5}{6} - 1\frac{1}{6} =$ ________

**31.** $\frac{4}{9} + 7\frac{7}{9} =$ ________

Name ____________________



# Relate Mixed Numbers and Decimals

Use the number line to write an equivalent mixed number or decimal for the given letter.

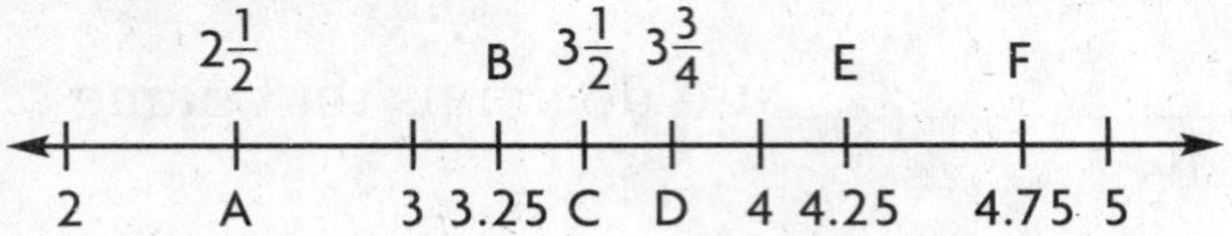


1. A ______  2. B ______  3. C ______

4. D ______  5. E ______  6. F ______

Write a decimal and a mixed number that are equivalent to each decimal model below.

7. 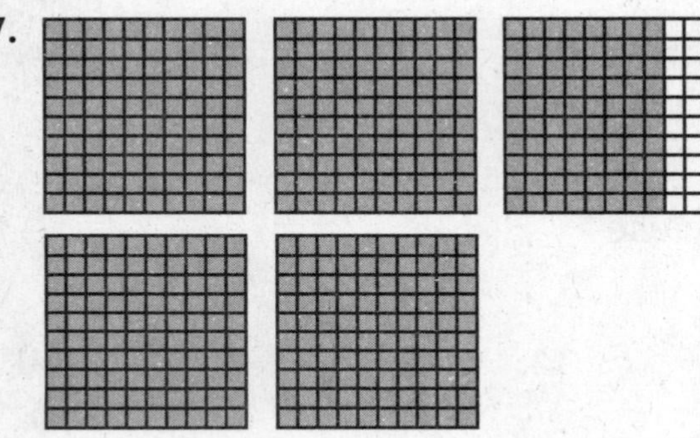

8. 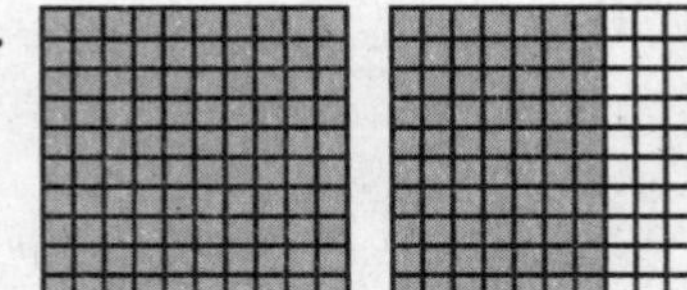

____________________  ____________________

Write an equivalent mixed number or decimal.

9. 12.75 ______  10. 5.50 ______  11. $6\frac{1}{5}$ ______

## Mixed Review

12. What digit is in the ten thousands place in the number 24,639?

____________________

13. These are Anna's spelling scores for 1 week: 86, 90, 85, 94, and 80. What is the median?

____________________

14. List the first 5 multiples of 3.

____________________

15. List the factors of 50.

____________________

Name ____________________



# Compare and Order Decimals

Compare. Write <, >, or = in each ◯.

1. 0.45 ◯ 0.35
2. 0.4 ◯ 0.6
3. 0.9 ◯ 0.91
4. 0.6 ◯ 0.64
5. 0.50 ◯ 0.55
6. 0.7 ◯ 0.17
7. 0.02 ◯ 0.22
8. 0.49 ◯ 0.4
9. 0.32 ◯ 0.23
10. 0.9 ◯ 0.99
11. 0.25 ◯ 0.205
12. 0.465 ◯ 0.437

Use the number line to order the decimals from *greatest* to *least*.

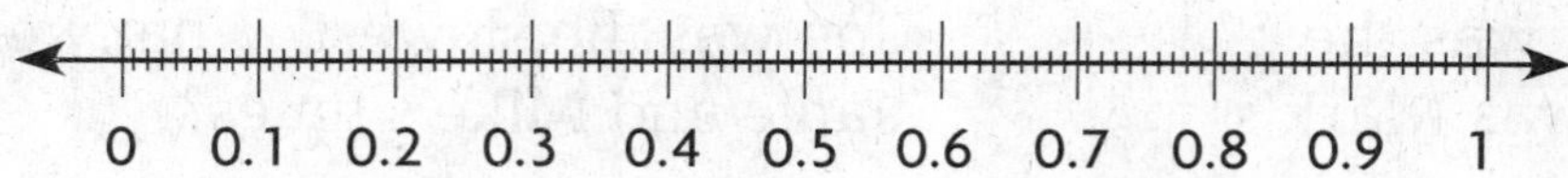


13. 0.45, 0.54, 0.40, 0.04 ____________________
14. 0.4, 0.5, 0.04, 0.05, 0.45 ____________________
15. 0.13, 0.31, 0.3, 0.01, 0.03 ____________________
16. 0.67, 0.7, 0.76, 0.07, 0.6 ____________________
17. 0.147, 0.243, 0.202, 0.215, 0.041 ____________________
18. 0.196, 0.204, 0.13, 0.092, 0.297 ____________________

## Mixed Review

19. Rosie's Umbrella Shop is selling umbrellas for $4.00 off the usual price of $15.00. What is the cost of buying 3 sale umbrellas?

____________________

20. To prepare for a presentation, Pete colored $\frac{1}{2}$ of a poster. Rebecca colored $\frac{1}{3}$ of the poster. What fraction still needs to be colored?

____________________

Write an equivalent decimal for each.

21. 0.4 __________
22. 0.60 __________
23. 0.8 __________
24. 0.7 __________

Name ______________________



# Problem Solving Strategy

## Use Logical Reasoning

Use logical reasoning to solve.

1. Mr. Berg's science class grew tomato plants. The recorded heights of the plants were 13 cm, 15 cm, 17 cm, and 20 cm. Jim's plant was the tallest. Steve's plant was 2 cm taller than Mark's. Eric's plant was the smallest. How tall was Mark's plant?

______________________

2. Four students ran a race in gym class. Erica had the fastest time of 10.5 seconds. The other recorded times were 13 seconds, 15 seconds and 20 seconds. Janie was slower than Erica, but faster than Mike. Joe was the slowest. What were Janie and Mike's times?

______________________

3. Stephanie's class took a spelling test. The scores were 90, 86, 89, 94, and 100. Stephanie got a higher grade than Mike. Sue scored 3 points higher than Joe. Ellen received the highest score. What was Stephanie's spelling grade?

______________________

4. The Nature Club recorded the number of birds at the bird feeder each day for a week. On Monday the club saw 15 birds. The numbers of birds at the feeder on the other days were 12, 13, 19, and 20. On Tuesday, the club saw the fewest birds. On Wednesday, the club saw fewer birds than on Monday. On Friday, the club saw the most birds. How many birds did the club see on Thursday ?

______________________

## Mixed Review

5. $\frac{1}{5} + \frac{2}{5} =$

______________________

6. List the factors of 21.

______________________

7. Order from *least* to *greatest*.
0.1, 3.00, 0.97, 0.08

______________________

8. 128 ÷ 8

______________________

# Round Decimals

Round each to the place of the underlined digit.

1. $\underline{6}.9$ ______
2. $\underline{7}.2$ ______
3. \$$8.\underline{3}2$ ______
4. $9.\underline{7}5$ ______
5. $5\underline{1}.2$ ______
6. $\underline{5}.964$ ______
7. \$$84.\underline{6}5$ ______
8. \$$\underline{5}.45$ ______

Round to the nearest whole number.

9. thirteen and eleven hundredths ______
10. six and ninety-five hundredths ______
11. ten and ninety-one hundredths ______
12. nine and forty-five hundredths ______

Round to the nearest hundredth.

13. 16.549 ______
14. 31.258 ______
15. 46.953 ______
16. 21.854 ______
17. 25.641 ______
18. 49.397 ______
19. 64.918 ______
20. 87.395 ______

## Mixed Review

21. $4.29 + $7.30
22. $6.14 + $0.88
23. $2.21 + $2.21
24. $48.19 + $27.55
25. $11.94 + $36.60
26. $8.79 − $0.56
27. $9.05 − $5.48
28. $7.12 − $6.81
29. $34.63 − $27.98
30. $59.99 − $ 5.90

31. Solve for $n$.
$540 \div n = 90$ ______

32. Solve for $n$.
$(64 - 5) + (12 \div 4) = n$ ______

Name ______________________________



# Estimate Sums and Differences

Estimate the sum or difference.

1. 1.5 + 1.2
2. 1.8 − 0.6
3. 2.3 − 0.7
4. 2.94 − 1.13
5. 23.94 + 16.98

6. 4.25 − 0.86
7. 6.45 − 2.63
8. \$5.62 + \$2.81
9. 16.95 − 3.29
10. 45.41 − 29.18

11. 1.62 − 1.34
12. 3.72 − 1.65
13. 2.36 − 1.74
14. 3.92 − 1.69
15. 3.45 + 2.07

16. 23.41 − 11.20
17. 2.53 + 1.56
18. 3.04 − 1.26
19. 2.82 + 2.35
20. 4.26 − 2.39

## Mixed Review

Write < or > in each ○.

21. \$8.15 + \$0.37 ○ \$8.50
22. \$19.00 ○ \$10.75 + \$9.00
23. \$6.59 + \$6.59 ○ \$13.20
24. \$7.43 + \$6.43 ○ \$13.90

For 25–26, use the table.

25. If you rounded all of the punt air times to the nearest second, what would be the time that occurred most often?

______________________________

26. Estimate the difference between Charley's longest time and his shortest time.

______________________________

| Charley's Football Punt Time in Air | |
|---|---|
| Monday | 3.4 seconds |
| Tuesday | 2.5 seconds |
| Wednesday | 1.7 seconds |
| Thursday | 2.8 seconds |
| Friday | 4.2 seconds |

Name ______________________



# Add and Subtract Decimals

Find the sum or difference. Estimate to check.

1. 4.90 + 3.41
2. 5.20 − 3.45
3. 5.00 − 2.49
4. 3.50 + 4.62
5. 35.91 + 4.00

6. 6.90 − 3.81
7. 10 − 4.632
8. 2.60 + 1.75
9. 5.428 + 1.735
10. 7.18 + 2.49

11. $5.98 − $0.50 ______
12. 35.846 − 4.9 ______
13. 12 − 5.913 ______

Find the missing number.

14. 3.62 − ■ = 1.5 ______
15. 4.96 − 1.2 = ■ ______
16. ■ + 0.29 = 3.81 ______

## Mixed Review

17. Sylvia ran 50 meters in 9.62 seconds. Linda finished 0.35 seconds later. Ramie's time was 0.09 seconds more than Linda's. What was Linda's time? Ramie's?

______

18. Henry bought radish, tomato, and pumpkin seed packages. The radish and tomato seed packages were $0.89 each. The pumpkin seed packages were $1.25 each. How many packages of each kind of seed did he buy if he spent $4.28 in all?

______

______

Multiply each number by 72.

19. 4 ______
20. 64 ______
21. 349 ______

Name ______________________________

# Problem Solving Skill

## Evaluate Reasonableness of Answers

**1.** Heidi works as a park ranger giving hiking tours. The trail is 4.3 miles long. If Heidi walks the trail 15 times each week, which is a reasonable estimate of the total number of miles she hikes?

**A** Heidi hiked 100 miles

**B** Heidi hiked 60 miles

**2.** Merrilyn is going to the market to buy produce. She needs 5 pounds of apples at $0.99 per pound and 9 pounds of green beans at $1.29 per pound. Which is a more reasonable estimate of how much money she should bring to the market?

**A** $14.00

**B** $32.00

For 3–4, use this information.

Peter is reading the instructions on how to build a birdhouse. He needs to cut some pieces of wood from a piece of lumber 100 cm long. The first piece should be 38.9 cm long; the second should be 22.5 cm long.

**3.** Which is the best estimate for the combined length of the two pieces he cuts?

**A** 70 cm **C** 30 cm

**B** 60 cm **D** 10 cm

**4.** Which is the best estimate for the length of the remaining lumber after Peter makes the two cuts?

**F** 40 cm **H** 15 cm

**G** 20 cm **J** 10 cm

## Mixed Review

**5.** Find the prime factors of 12. ____________

**6.** List 3 multiples of 10. ____________

**7.** Write the fact family for 3, 5, and 15. ______________________________

**8.** $\begin{array}{r} 90{,}005 \\ -\ 5{,}842 \\ \hline \end{array}$

**9.** $\frac{9}{10} - \frac{3}{5} =$ ______

**10.** $\begin{array}{r} 52 \\ \times\ 81 \\ \hline \end{array}$

Name ___________________________________________



# Choose the Appropriate Unit

## Vocabulary

Complete.

1. Measuring length, width, height, and distance are all forms of ______________ measurement.

2. A(n) ______________ is about the length of a baseball bat.

3. A(n) ______________ is about the distance you can walk in 20 minutes.

4. A(n) ______________ is about the height of a cat.

5. A(n) ______________ is about the length of your thumb from the first knuckle to the tip.

---

Choose the most reasonable unit of measure. Write *in.*, *ft*, *yd*, or *mi*.

6. The length of a calculator is about 4 _________.

7. The height of a flagpole is about 25 _________.

8. The height of a refrigerator is about 2 _________.

9. The distance along the walkathon is 12 _________.

Write the greater measurement.

10. 50 ft or 50 yd _________

11. 17 mi or 17 yd _________

12. 243 in. or 243 yd _________



## Mixed Review

13. $\frac{1}{6} + \frac{2}{3}$ _________

14. $\frac{5}{6} + \frac{2}{3}$ _________

15. Write $\frac{10}{15}$ as a fraction in simplest form. _________

Name ______________________



# Measure Fractional Parts

Estimate to the nearest inch. Then measure to the nearest $\frac{1}{8}$ inch.

1.

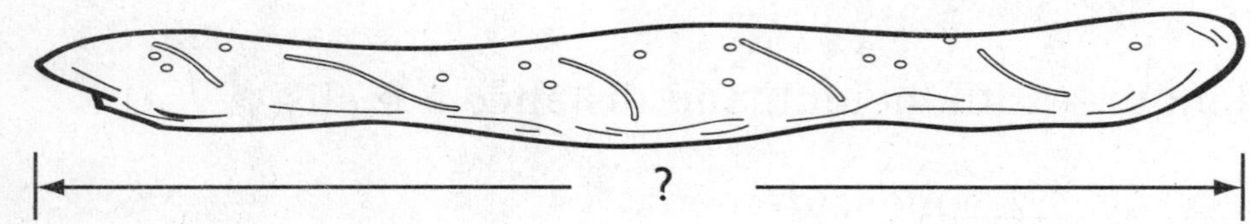


______________________

Estimate to the nearest inch. Then measure to the nearest $\frac{1}{4}$ inch.

2.

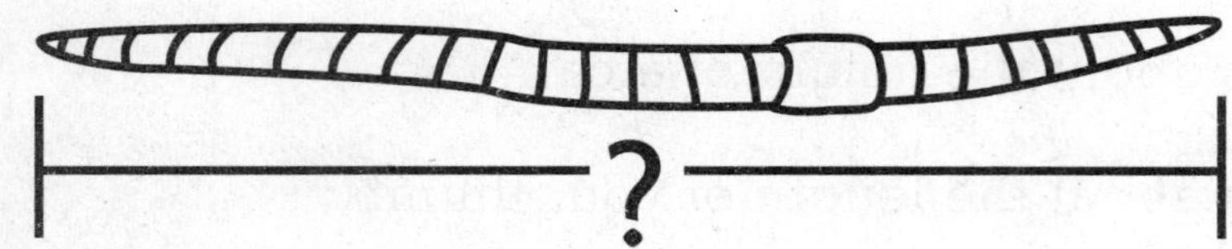


______________________

Order the measurements from *least* to *greatest.*

3. $4\frac{1}{8}$ in.; $3\frac{1}{2}$ in.; $4\frac{1}{4}$ in.; $4\frac{3}{8}$ in.

______________________

4. $\frac{1}{8}$ in.; $\frac{1}{2}$ in.; $\frac{3}{4}$ in.; $\frac{5}{8}$ in.

______________________

## Mixed Review

For 5–6, use the Tree Growth Chart.

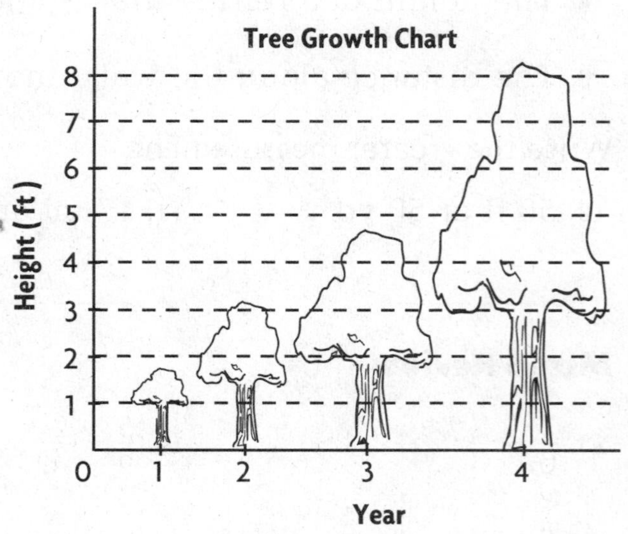


5. To the nearest foot, how tall was the tree in the first year? second year? third year? fourth year?

______________________

6. Between which two years did the tree grow the most?

______________________

______________________

Name ______________________



# Algebra: Change Linear Units

Complete. Tell whether you multiply or divide.

1. 48 in. = ______ ft
______
2. 36 ft = ______ yd
______
3. 4 yd = ______ in.
______

4. 3 mi = ______ ft
______
5. 3,520 yd = ______ mi
______
6. 5 mi = ______ ft
______

7. 7 ft = ______ in.
______
8. 300 ft = ______ yd
______
9. 432 in. = ______ yd
______

Write an equation that can be used to complete each table.
Complete the table.

10.

| Feet, $f$ | 3 | 6 | | 12 | 15 |
|---|---|---|---|---|---|
| Yards, $y$ | 1 | | 3 | | 5 |

______

11.

| Yards, $y$ | 1,760 | | |
|---|---|---|---|
| Miles, $m$ | 1 | 3 | 4 |

______

Compare. Write <, >, or = in the ◯.

12. 38 in. ◯ 3 ft
13. 10,000 ft ◯ 4 mi
14. 100 in. ◯ 3 yd

## Mixed Review

Add or subtract.

15. $5{,}283 + 467$
16. $3{,}512 - 468$
17. $7{,}536 - 207$
18. $4{,}106 - 314$

19. $5{,}490 - 83$
20. $6{,}372 + 891$
21. $7{,}536 + 18$
22. $2{,}013 - 5$

Name ________________________________



# Capacity

## Vocabulary

Complete.

1. ____________ is the amount a container can hold when filled.

2. Write the word *cup, pint, quart,* or *gallon* to label each container.

____________ ____________ ____________ ____________

---

Complete the tables. Change the units.

3.

| Cup | Pint |
|---|---|
| 4 | |
| 8 | |
| | 8 |

4.

| Pint | Quart |
|---|---|
| 4 | |
| | 3 |
| 8 | |

5.

| Quart | Gallon |
|---|---|
| 8 | |
| 12 | |
| | 4 |

Choose the unit of capacity. Write *cup, pint, quart,* or *gallon.*

6. 

____________

7. 

____________

8. 

____________

## Mixed Review

Round the number to the greatest place value.

9. 3,654 ____________ 10. 4,399 ____________ 11. 2,543 ____________

12. 17,536 ____________ 13. 213,502 ____________ 14. 109,563 ____________

Name ______________________



# Weight

## Vocabulary

Complete.

1. A bread truck weighs about 1 __________.
2. A slice of bread weighs about 1 __________.
3. A loaf of bread weighs about 1 __________.

---

Circle the more reasonable measurement.

4. 1,200 lb or 1,200 oz
5. 10 T or 10 lb
6. 68 oz or 68 lb

Complete.

7. 2 lb = ________ oz
8. 4 T = ________ lb
9. 60,000 lb = ________ T
10. 64 oz = ________ lb
11. 1 T = ________ oz
12. 208 oz = ________ lb

Write *3 lb, 5,000 lb, 1,000 lb,* or *35 oz* to make each of the following true.

13. 3 lb > ______________
14. 2T < ______________
15. 5 lb < ______________
16. 17 lb > ______________

## Mixed Review

Write the product or quotient.

17. $6 \times 3 =$ ________
18. $10 \times 3 =$ ________
19. $6 \times 5 =$ ________
20. $35 \div 7 =$ ________
21. $7 \times 6 =$ ________
22. $18 \div 3 =$ ________
23. $7 \times 8 =$ ________
24. $36 \div 6 =$ ________
25. $8 \times 11 =$ ________

Name ______________________________



# Problem Solving Strategy

## Compare Strategies

Choose a strategy to solve.

1. Sarah is making a large pot of soup. She adds 7 quarts of water and 3 pints of tomato juice. How many one-pint servings can she make?

   ______________________________

2. Along the 30-foot wall, there is a plant every 6 feet. The plants start at one end of the wall. How many plants are there?

   ______________________________

3. Roland is buying sod for some patches on his lawn. Each patch needs 4 feet of sod. He buys 5 yards of sod. How many patches can he cover?

   ______________________________

4 Karla is making tea for some friends. Each cup of tea uses 1 cup of water. Karla fills a 3-quart pitcher with water. How many teacups can she fill?

   ______________________________

5. Cherie's town is bagging aluminum cans for recycling. Each bag holds 5 pounds of cans. They need to collect 2 tons of cans before their donation will be accepted. How many bags of cans will they need?

   ______________________________

6. Henry collected 10 cans in the first hour, 15 cans the second hour, and 20 cans the third hour. If this pattern continues, how many cans will he collect in all in six hours?

   ______________________________

## Mixed Review

Write the product or sum.

7. $\begin{array}{r} 314 \\ \times \quad 4 \\ \hline \end{array}$

8. $\begin{array}{r} 236 \\ \times \quad 3 \\ \hline \end{array}$

9. $\begin{array}{r} 413 \\ + \quad 37 \\ \hline \end{array}$

10. $\begin{array}{r} 207 \\ \times \quad 4 \\ \hline \end{array}$

11. $\begin{array}{r} 535 \\ + 493 \\ \hline \end{array}$

12. $\begin{array}{r} 537 \\ + 395 \\ \hline \end{array}$

13. $\begin{array}{r} 537 \\ \times \quad 5 \\ \hline \end{array}$

14. $\begin{array}{r} 716 \\ + 239 \\ \hline \end{array}$

15. $\begin{array}{r} 716 \\ \times \quad 9 \\ \hline \end{array}$

16. $\begin{array}{r} 375 \\ + 909 \\ \hline \end{array}$

Name ______________________________



# Linear Measure

## Vocabulary

Complete.

1. A ______________ is about the width of your index finger.

2. A ______________ is equal to 10 centimeters and is about the width of an adult's hand.

3. A ______________ is about the distance from one hand to the other when you stretch out your arms.

4. A ______________ is about the length of 10 football fields.

---

Use a centimeter ruler or a meterstick to measure each item. Write the measurement and unit of measure used.

5. length of your desk ______________

6. width of a piece of chalk ______________

7. height of a tree ______________

Choose the most reasonable unit of measure. Write *a, b,* or *c.*

8. _____ width of a head  a. 2 km  b. 2 dm  c. 2 m

9. _____ distance around the school  a. 1,000 cm  b. 1,000 km  c. 1,000 m

10. _____ height of a tree  a. 5 km  b. 5 dm  c. 5 m

11. _____ distance between two towns  a. 22 km  b. 22 dm  c. 22 m



## Mixed Review

12. $15 \times 10$

13. $1{,}000 \times 12$

14. $14.3 - 7.6$

15. $13.4 + 16.6$

16. $350 \times n = 35{,}000$  $n =$ _____

17. $n \times 36 = 360$  $n =$ _____

Name ____________________



# Algebra: Change Linear Units

Complete.

1. 300 cm = ________ m
2. 3 km = ________ m
3. 4,000 m = ________ km
4. 50 m = ________ dm
5. 40 km = ________ m
6. 68 m = ________ cm

Write the correct unit.

7. 500 cm = ________ m
8. 60 dm = ________ m
9. 8 ________ = 8,000 m
10. 20 cm = ________ dm
11. 3,000 m = 3 ________
12. 200 m = ________ cm

Compare. Write $>$, $<$, or $=$.

13. 12 m ________ 120 cm
14. 14 m ________ 1,400 cm
15. 3 km ________ 4,000 m
16. 4 m ________ 3 km
17. 30 dm ________ 3 m
18. 300 m ________ 3,000 dm

Order from least to greatest.

19. 2m; 100 cm; 4 dm; 3 km

________________________

20. 3,000 m; 3 dm; 300 km; 3,000 cm

________________________

## Mixed Review

21. Which customary unit of length would be best to give the distance across a soccer field?

________________________

22. Write an expression for 3 times the number of people, *p*, at the county fair.

________________________

23. $84 \times 62$

24. $48{,}588 - 40{,}315$

25. $315 \times 27$

26. $4\overline{)3{,}788}$

27. $6\overline{)973}$

28. $8\overline{)5{,}800}$

29. $12\overline{)144}$

30. $4\overline{)3604}$

Name ______________________________



# Capacity

## Vocabulary

Complete.

1. A ____________ is about the size of a sports-drink bottle. It contains 1,000 milliliters.

2. A ____________ is about the size of a drop of liquid in an eyedropper.

Choose the more reasonable unit of measure. Write *mL* or *L*.

3. wading pool ____________

4. a soda can ____________

5. a baby bottle ____________

Choose the best estimate. Circle *a, b,* or *c.*

6. 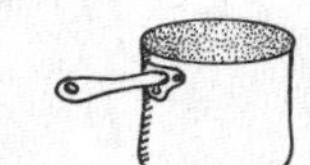
a. 3 mL
b. 30 mL
c. 3 L

7. 
a. 42 mL
b. 420 mL
c. 42 L

8. 
a. 62 mL
b. 620 mL
c. 62 L

Change to milliliters or liters.

9. 5 L = ________ mL

10. 70 L = ________ mL

11. 4 L = ________ mL

12. 6,000 mL = ________ L

13. 12,000 mL = ________ L

14. 26,000 mL = ________ L

## Mixed Review

15. $\begin{array}{r} 187 \\ +435 \\ \hline \end{array}$

16. $\begin{array}{r} 461 \\ \times\ 34 \\ \hline \end{array}$

17. $4\overline{)723}$

18. $5\frac{3}{16} + 7\frac{1}{16}$

19. Ron's car has a 12-gallon gas tank. If gas costs $1.45 per gallon, how much will it cost to fill the tank?

____________________

20. A 5-lb bag of flour costs $1.10. A 20-oz bag of flour costs $0.40. Which is the better buy?

____________________

21. 5 km = ________ m

22. 71 m = ________ cm

23. 98 m = ________ dm

Name ____________________

# Mass

## Vocabulary

Write the letter of the word that is best described.

1. ______ the amount of mass that is about equal to a baseball bat
2. ______ the amount of matter in an object
3. ______ the amount of mass that is about equal to a large paper clip

a. kilogram (kg)
b. gram (g)
c. mass

---

Choose the more reasonable measurement.

4. 
1 g or 1 kg
________

5. 

5 g or 5 kg
________

6. 

200 g or 20 kg
________

7. 
600 g or 600 kg
________

Change to grams.

8. 3 kg = ________ g
9. 14 kg = ________ g
10. 20 kg = ________ g

## Mixed Review

11. One serving of macaroni and cheese is 70 g. How many kilograms are needed to serve 200 people?

________________________

12. If 3 servings of macaroni and cheese cost $0.99, how much will it cost to serve 200 people?

________________________

13. $72\overline{)4,216}$
14. $19\overline{)103}$
15. $10\overline{)20,000}$
16. $24\overline{)1920}$

Name ____________________



# Problem Solving Strategy

## Draw a Diagram

Draw a diagram to solve.

1. Steve and Sara bought a total of 14 items at the grocery store. Sara bought two more than twice the number of items that Steve bought. How many items did each buy?

______________________

______________________

______________________

2. Mike, Thea, and Emily were reading library books. Mike read 4 books. Thea read 2 more than twice the number of books that Emily read. Emily read 1 book less than Mike. How many books did each person read?

______________________

______________________

______________________

3. Tina, Kevin, and Amy flew their kites. Kevin's kite flew 2 meters higher than Amy's. Tina's flew 1 meter lower than half as high as Amy's. Amy's kite flew 300 decimeters high. How high did Tina's and Kevin's kites fly?

______________________

______________________

______________________

4. Jim's family went hiking. Jim was able to hike 5 miles. His mother and father each hiked 1 mile more than three times the distance that Jim hiked. Jim's brother Tim hiked 1 mile less than Jim did. How far did each person hike?

______________________

______________________

______________________

## Mixed Review

5. 300 m = ________ cm

6. 400 dm = ________ m

7. 7,000 m = ________ km

8. 20 ft = ________ in.

9. 4 lb = ________ oz

10. 1 pt = ________ c

11. 48 in. = ________ ft

12. 6 c = ________ pt

13. 20 qt = ________ gal

Name ______________________



# Perimeter of Polygons

Name the polygon. Find the perimeter.

1. 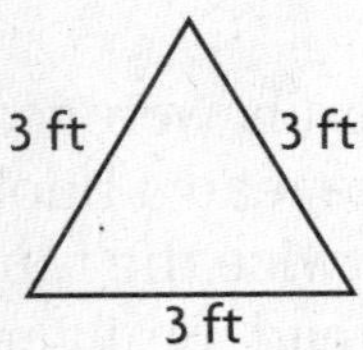


2. 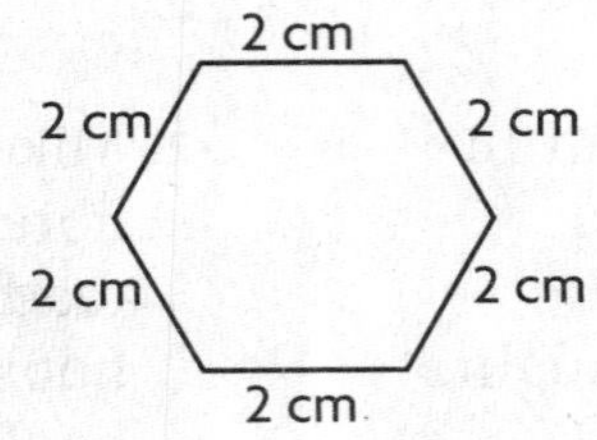


3. 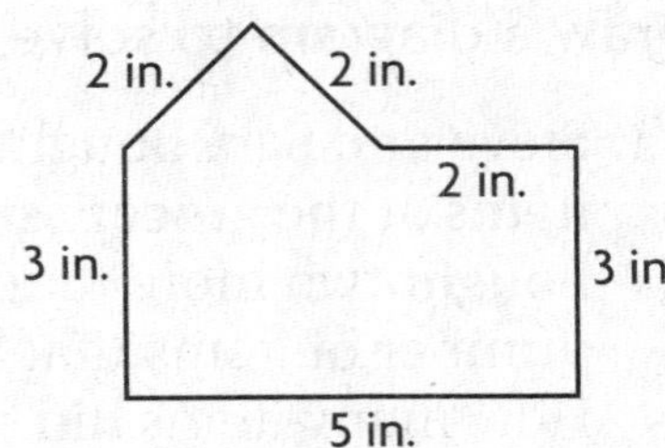


______ ______ ______

4. 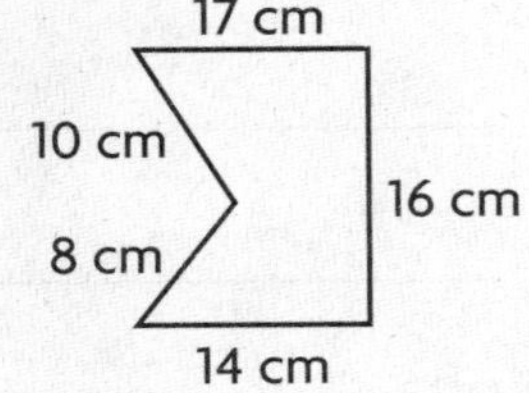


5. 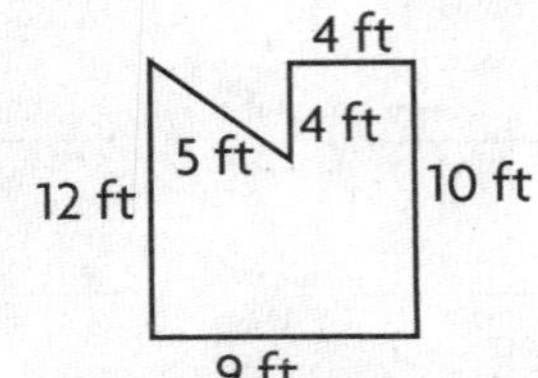


6. 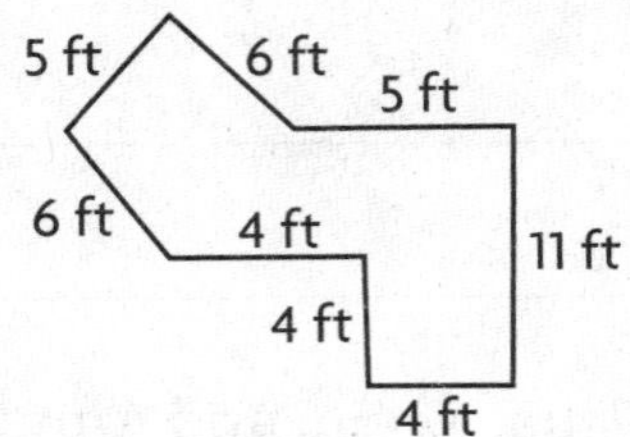


______ ______ ______

Find the perimeter.

7. 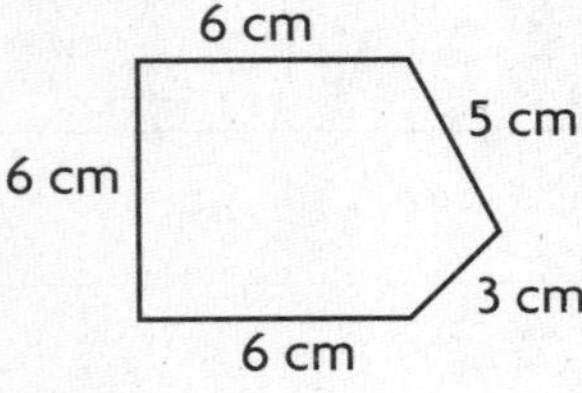


8. 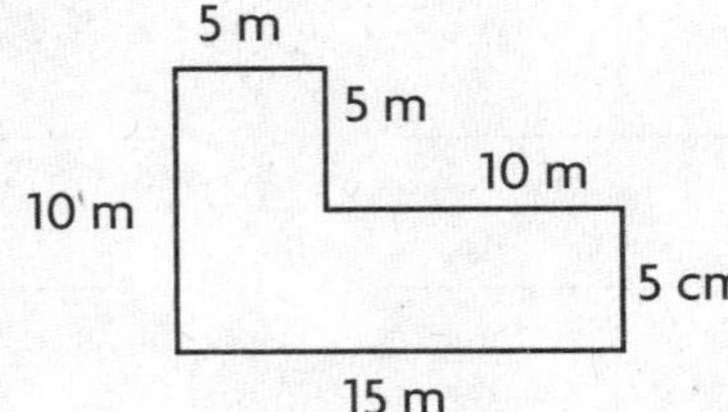


9. 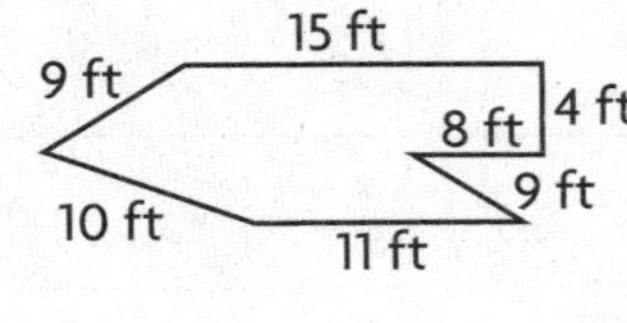


______ ______ ______

## Mixed Review

10. $871 - 323$

11. $165 - 84$

12. $3,284 - 189$

13. $5,831 - 428$

14. $2,179 - 871$

15. $\frac{4}{5} - \frac{2}{10} =$ ______

16. $\frac{11}{12} - \frac{3}{4} =$ ______

17. $\frac{9}{15} - \frac{1}{5} =$ ______

Name ____________________



# Estimate and Find Perimeter

## Vocabulary

Fill in the blank to complete the sentence.

1. ____________ is the distance around a polygon.

Use a formula to find the perimeter.

2. Rectangle: 6 mi, 3 mi, 3 mi, 6 mi

____________

3. Square: 4 ft, 4 ft, 4 ft, 4 ft

____________

4. 4 km, 4 km, 3 km, 1 km, 7 km

____________

5. 6 in., 4 in., 4 in., 8 in.

____________

6. 5 m, 5 m, 5 m, 5 m, 5 m

____________

7. 14 yd, 5 yd, 5 yd, 14 yd

____________

8. 8 ft, 8 ft, 8 ft, 8 ft

____________

9. 10 yd, 10 yd, 10 yd

____________

10. 8 cm, 8 cm, 2 cm, 2 cm, 12 cm

____________

## Mixed Review

11. $\frac{3}{9} + \frac{2}{9} =$ ____

12. $\frac{1}{8} + \frac{5}{8} =$ ____

13. $\frac{9}{10} - \frac{5}{10} =$ ____

14. $\frac{5}{7} - \frac{3}{7} =$ ____

15. $12\overline{)780}$

16. $19\overline{)1,862}$

17. $8\overline{)4,963}$

18. $17\overline{)3,727}$

Name ______________________________



# Estimate and Find Area

Find the area.

1.

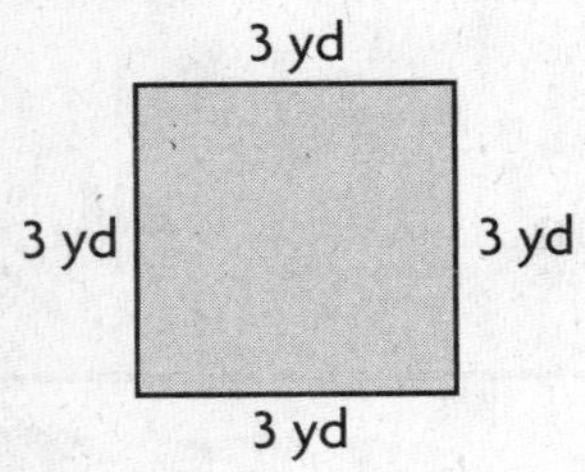


______________

2.

4 cm
1 cm
1 cm
4 cm

______________

3.

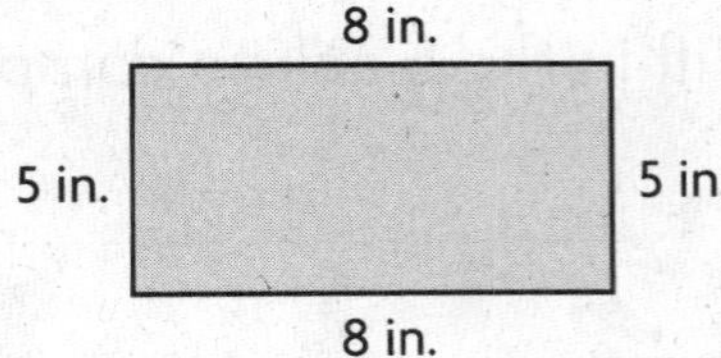


______________

4.

6 m
2 m
2 m
6 m

______________

5.

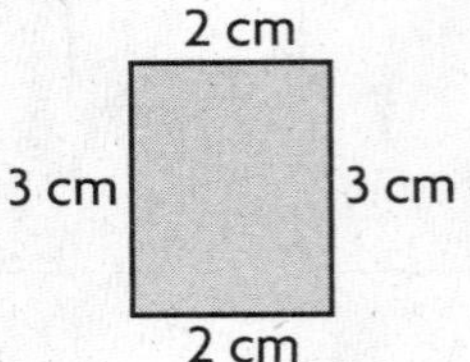


______________

6.

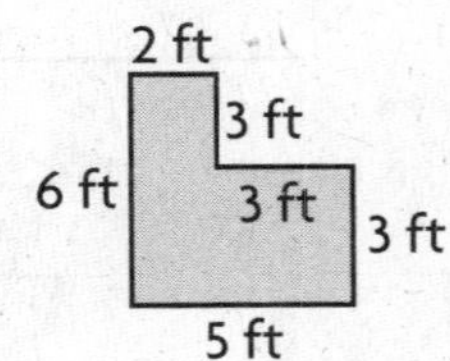


______________

7.

2 ft
2 ft
2 ft
2 ft
4 ft
2 ft
4 ft
6 ft

______________

8.

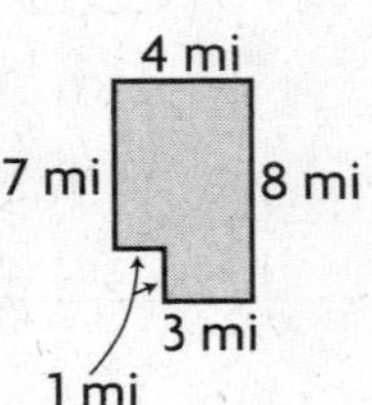


______________

9.

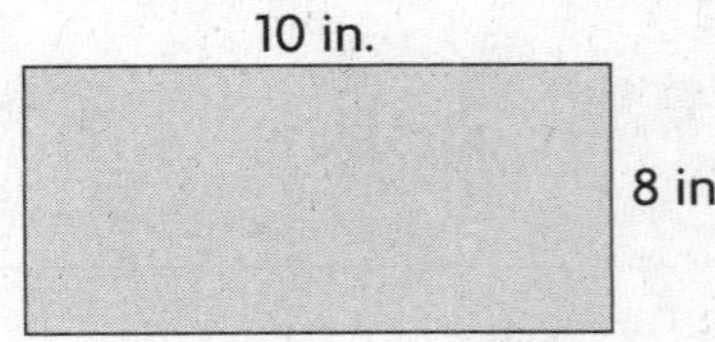


______________

## Mixed Review

10. $67 \times 16$

11. $627 \times 41$

12. $129 \times 76$

13. $492 \times 10$

14. $412 \times 89$

15. $871 \times 13$

16. $165 \times 64$

17. $52 \times 37$

18. $69 \times 28$

19. $955 \times 31$

20. $(7 \times 3) - (4 \times 4) =$ ______

21. $(12 \times 3) - 15 =$ ______

22. $(19 + 28) - (8 \times 2) =$ ______

23. $(17 - 7) + (5 \times 5) =$ ______

Name ______________________________



# Relate Area and Perimeter

Write the area and the perimeter.

**1.** 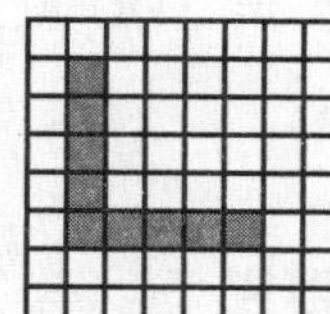

______________

**2.** 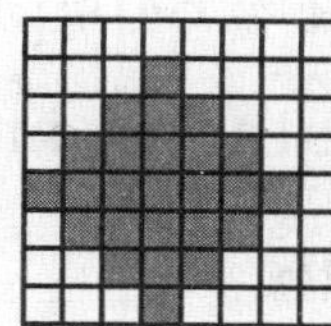

______________

**3.** 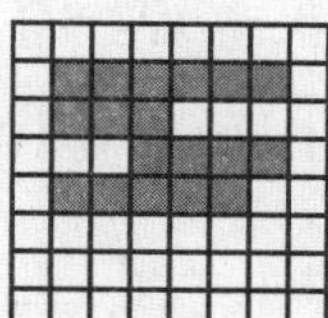

______________

For 4–6, find the area and perimeter of each figure. Then draw another figure that has the same area but a different perimeter.

**4.** 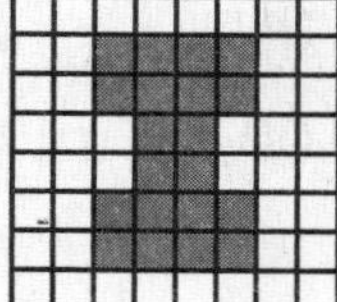

______________

**5.** 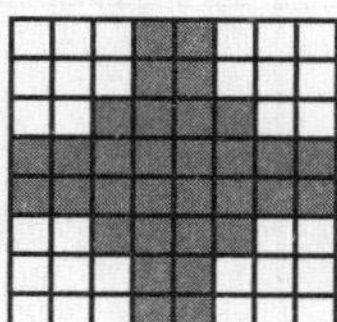

______________

**6.** 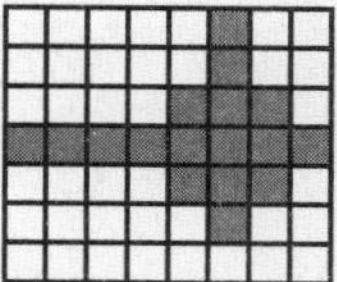 

______________

**7.** Which of the figures a–d below have the same area but different perimeters?

______________

**8.** Which of the figures a–d below have the same perimeter but different areas?

______________

**a.** 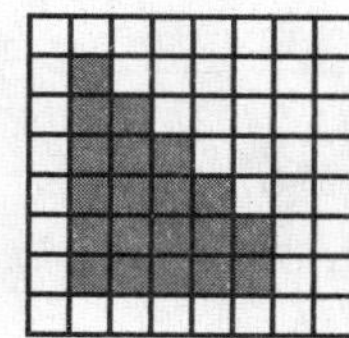

**b.** 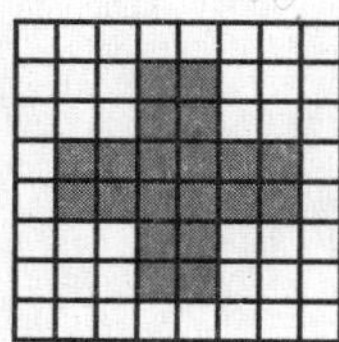

**c.** 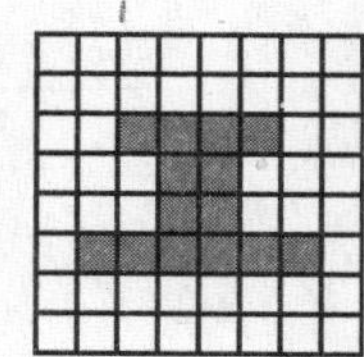

**d.** 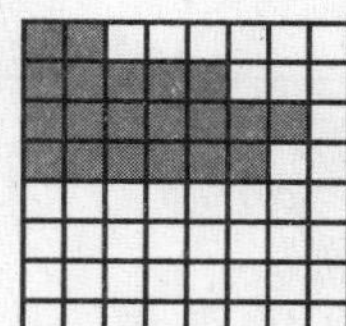

## Mixed Review

**9.** $7\frac{1}{2} + 3\frac{9}{12} =$ ______

**10.** $4\frac{4}{9} - 1\frac{1}{5} =$ ______

**11.** $10\frac{6}{7} - 5\frac{2}{14} =$ ______

Circle the prime numbers.

**12.** 17 33 39 5 142 29 47 30 111 13 52 56 11

Name ______________________________

# Relate Formulas and Rules

Complete for each rectangle.

1. Area = 20 sq in.
   Length = 4 in.
   Width = ______

2. Area = 64 sq mi
   Length = 4 mi
   Width = ______

3. Area = 100 sq m
   Width = 4 m
   Length = ______

Find the unknown length.

4. 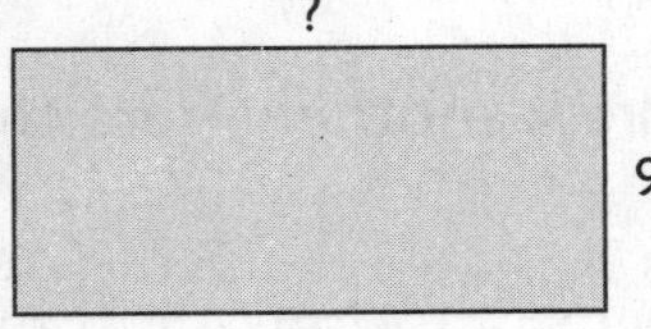


Area = 108 sq cm

______

5. 16 yd

?

Area = 80 sq yd

______

6. 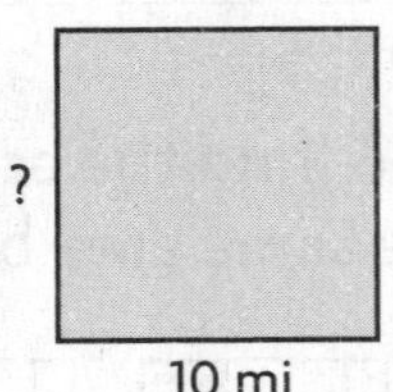


Area = 100 sq mi

______

7. 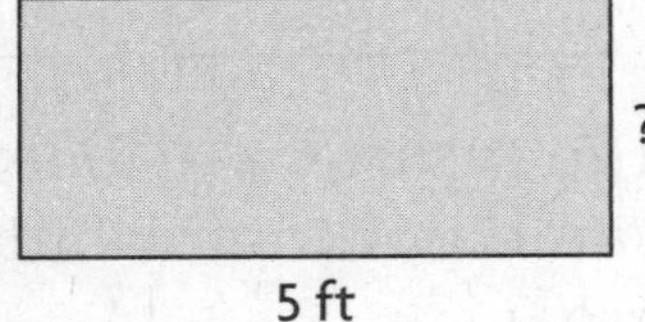


Perimeter = 18 ft

______

8. 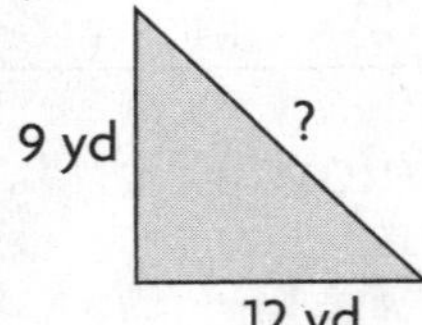


Perimeter = 36 yd

______

9. 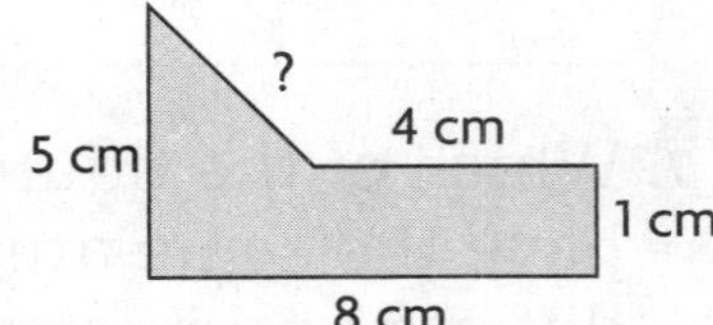


Perimeter = 24 cm

______

## Mixed Review

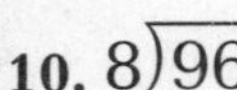

10. $8\overline{)96}$ 11. $3\overline{)42}$ 12. $5\overline{)90}$ 13. $9\overline{)207}$ 14. $2\overline{)58}$

15. $12\overline{)300}$ 16. $18\overline{)144}$ 17. $6\overline{)246}$ 18. $11\overline{)231}$ 19. $18\overline{)270}$

Name ______________________________________________



# Problem Solving Strategy

## Find a Pattern

Use *find a pattern* to solve.

1. Alexis is going to put carpet in three rectangular rooms in her house. How do the areas of the rooms change if each room is two times as long and three times as wide as the one before it? Make a table to show how the areas change. Then solve.

   Room 1: $l = 4$ yd, $w = 2$ yd

   Room 2: $l = 8$ yd, $w = 6$ yd

   Room 3: $l = 16$ yd, $w = 18$ yd

______________________________________________

2. Douglas has different sizes of rectangular picture frames. How does the perimeter change for each of his picture frames when the width increases by 5 inches? Complete the table and solve.

| Picture Frame Sizes | | | |
|---|---|---|---|
| | Length (in.) | Width (in.) | Perimeter (in.) |
| Frame A | 12 | 10 | |
| Frame B | 12 | 15 | |
| Frame C | 12 | 20 | |
| Frame D | 12 | 25 | |

______________________________________________

## Mixed Review

3. $15 \times 7 =$ ______ 4. $121 \div 11 =$ ______ 5. $42 \times 8 =$ ______

Name ____________________

# Faces, Edges, and Vertices

Which solid figure do you see in each?

1. 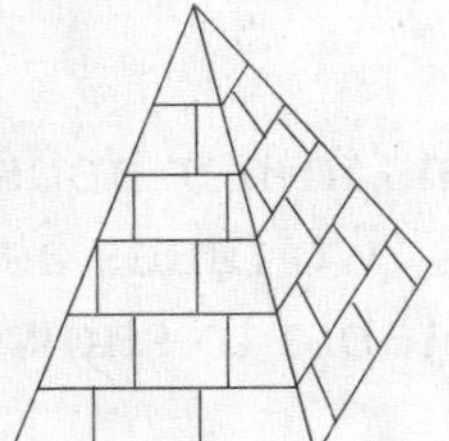

2. 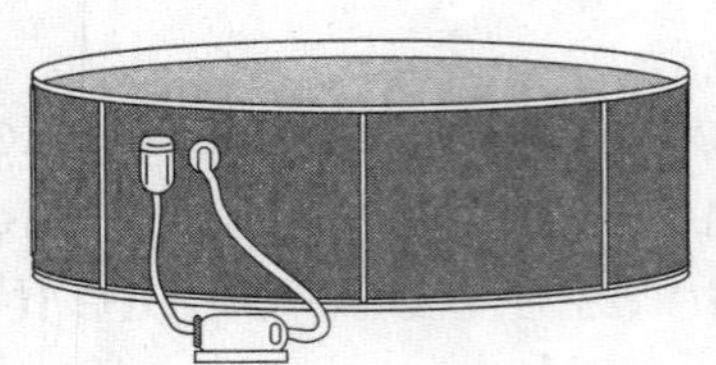

3. 

____________________ ____________________ ____________________

Copy the drawings. Circle each vertex, outline each edge in red, and shade one face in yellow.

4. 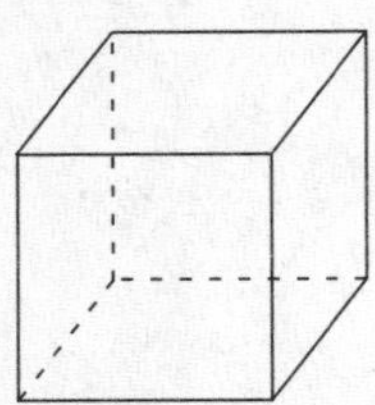

5. 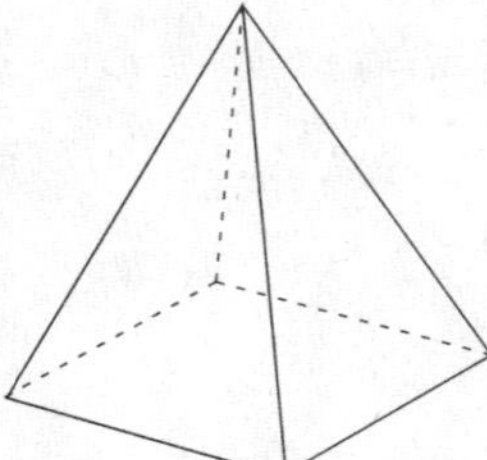

6. 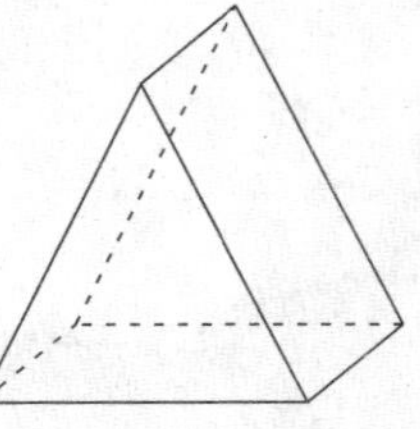

Write the names of the faces and the number of each kind of face of the solid figure.

7. triangular pyramid

8. triangular prism

9. square pyramid

____________________ ____________________ ____________________

____________________ ____________________ ____________________

## Mixed Review

Find the perimeter of each figure.

10. 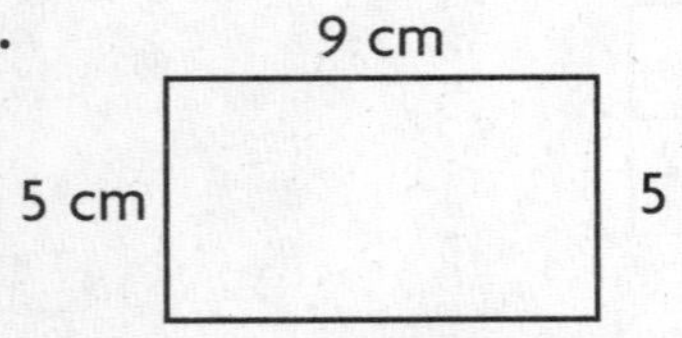


11. 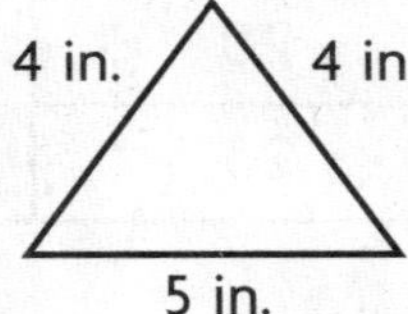


12. 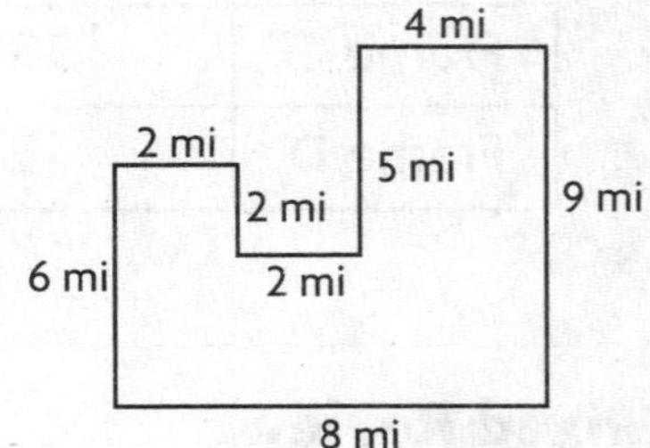


____________________ ____________________ ____________________

Name ____________________



# Patterns for Solid Figures

## Vocabulary

Fill in the blank.

1. A ________ is a two-dimensional pattern of a three-dimensional figure.

---

Write the letter of the figure that is made with each net.

2. 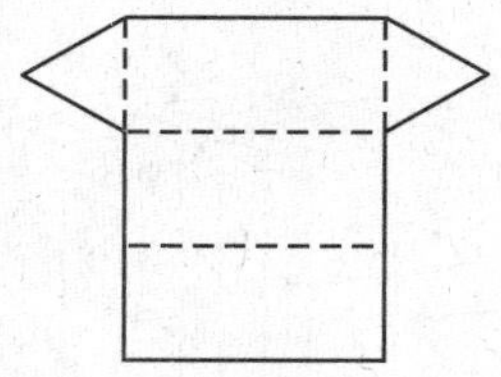

3. 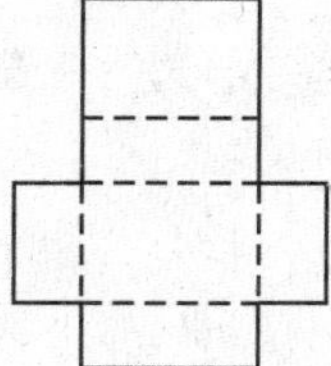

4. 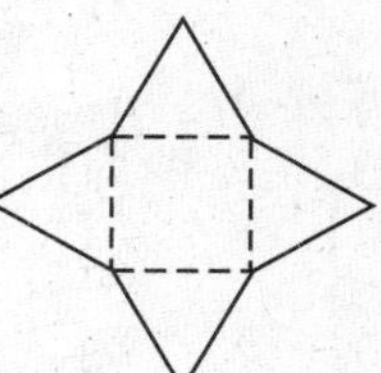

5. 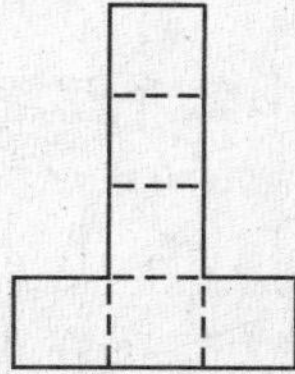

a. 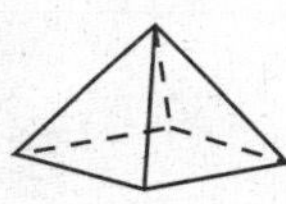

b. 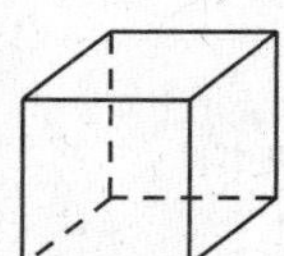

c. 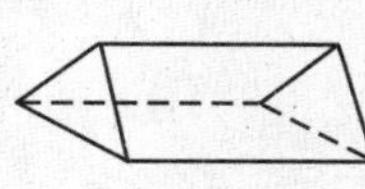

d. 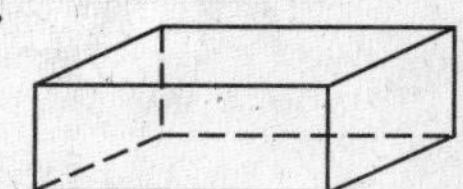

6. Which of the following nets would make a rectangular prism?

a. 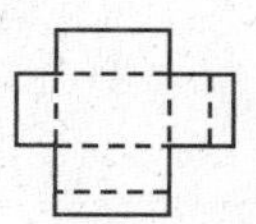

b. 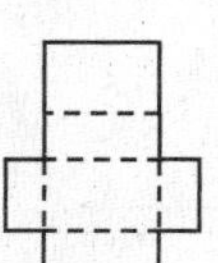

c. 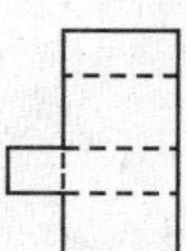

d. 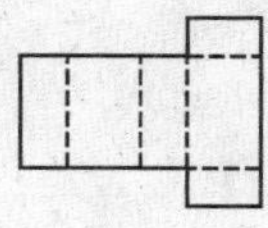

________________________________

## Mixed Review

7. $10\overline{)1{,}000}$

8. $14\overline{)0}$

9. $25\overline{)475}$

10. $32\overline{)256}$

11. Franz ate $1\frac{3}{8}$ granola bars. Aimee ate $2\frac{1}{8}$ snack bars. How many granola bars did Franz and Aimee eat in all?

________________________________

Name ______________________



# Estimate and Find Volume of Prisms

Find the volume.

1. 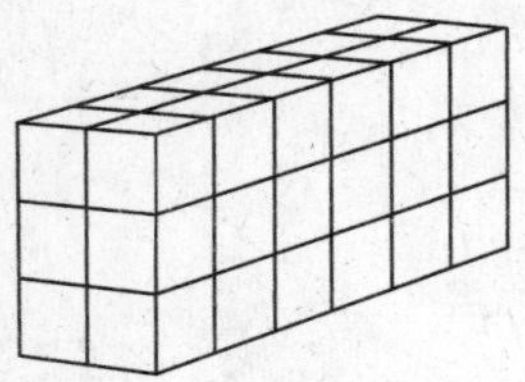

______________

2. 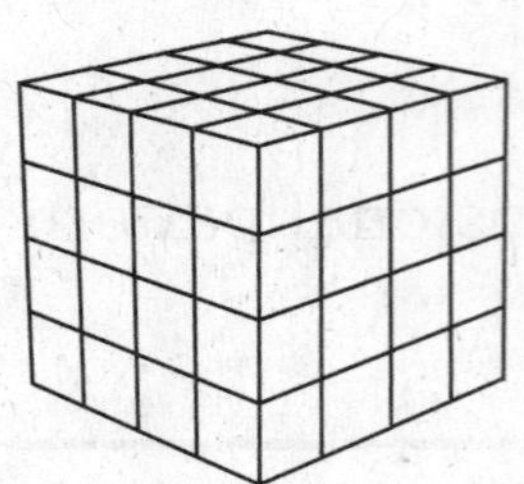

______________

3. 

______________

4. 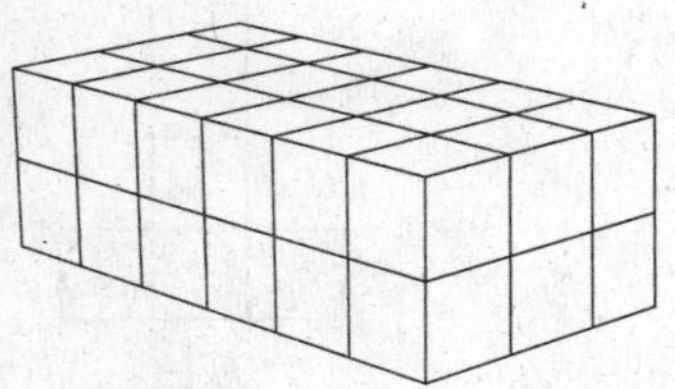

______________

5. 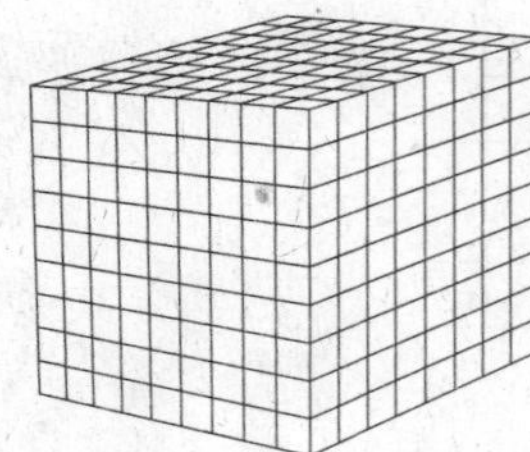

______________

6. 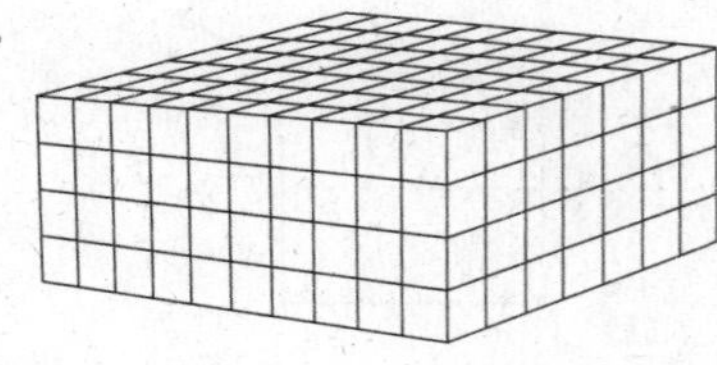

______________

7. 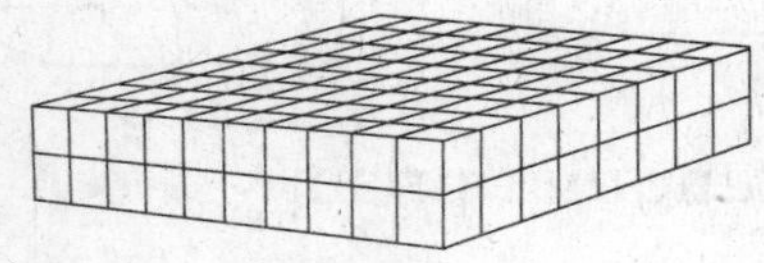

______________

8. 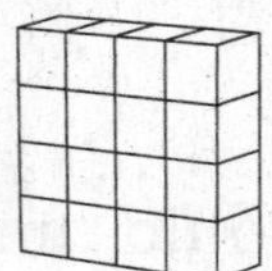

______________

9. 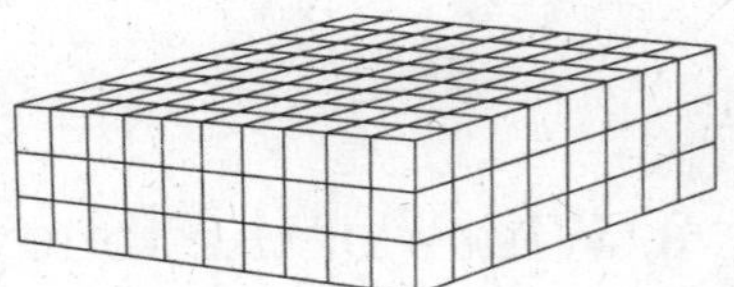

______________

## Mixed Review

10. $17 \times 6$

11. $247 \times 48$

12. $89 \times 17$

13. $478 \times 45$

14. $112 \times 39$

15. $222 \times 31$

16. $52 \times 44$

17. $63 \times 12$

18. $678 \times 18$

19. $456 \times 48$

20. $75 \times 36$

21. $67 \times 58$

22. $159 \times 43$

23. $517 \times 62$

24. $802 \times 24$

Name ______________________________



# Problem Solving Skill: Too Much/Too Little Information

Decide if the problem has *too much* or *too little information.* Then solve the problem if possible.

1. There are 90 rocks in Joe's box. He has 45 different kinds of rocks in his box. The box is 12 inches long, 6 inches wide, and 4 inches high. What is the volume of the box of rocks?

_______________

2. Klamo likes to take pictures of animals in her backyard. She has over 100 pictures of animals. She keeps her pictures in a box that is 1 foot high. What is the volume of the box?

_______________

3. Spencer puts corn from his garden into wooden boxes. Each box contains 30 ears of corn. Each box is 2 meters long and 1 meter wide. What is the volume of the wooden box?

_______________

4. A cereal box weighs 1 pound. It is 12 inches high, 6 inches long, and 2 inches wide. What is the volume of the cereal box?

_______________

## Mixed Review

Find the area and perimeter of each.

5. 16 ft, 9 ft

_______________

6. 9 cm, 4 cm

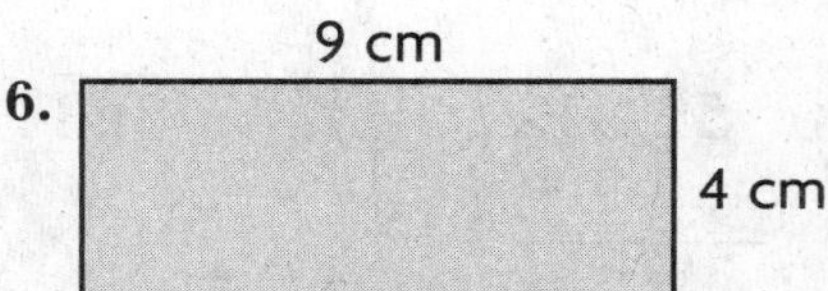

_______________

7. 18 mi, 23 mi

_______________

Name ______________________________ LESSON 27.1

## Record Outcomes

For 1–4, use the table.

Don and Carol organized their outcomes in this table. They used the 3-letter spinner and the 4-number spinner shown.

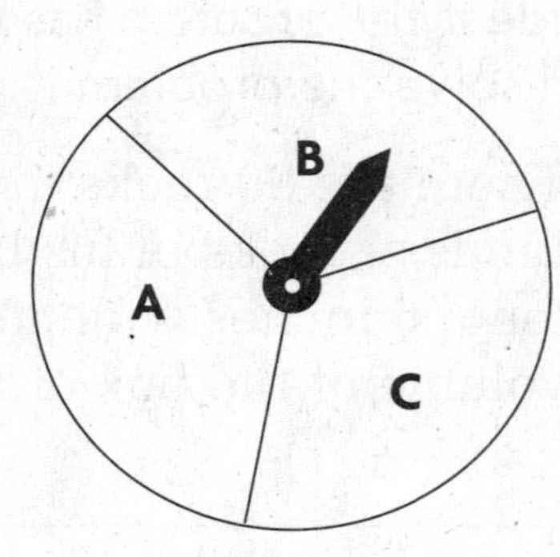


| Number | Letter A | Letter B | Letter C |
|---|---|---|---|
| 1 | II | | I |
| 2 | | III | |
| 3 | I | | I |
| 4 | IIII | | II |

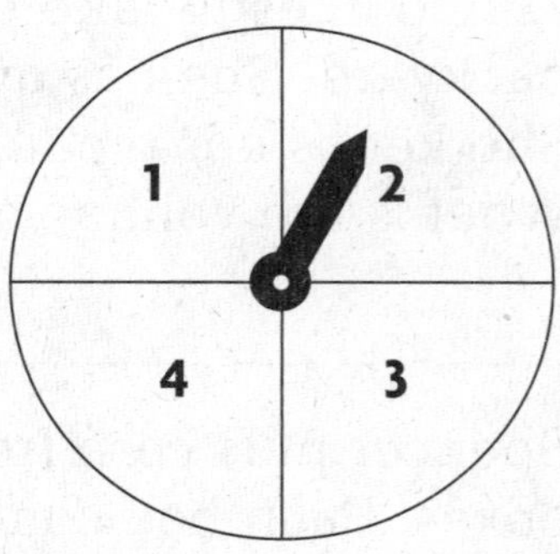


1. Name all the possible outcomes for this experiment.

______________________________

______________________________

2. How many possible outcomes are there?

______________________________

3. How many outcomes would there be if they had used a 4-letter spinner?

______________________________

4. In Don and Carol's experiment which outcome occurred most often?

______________________________

**Mixed Review**

5. 318,849 + 984,741

6. 52,842 × 6

7. 17)893

8. $\frac{5}{12} - \frac{1}{4} =$ ______

9. $\frac{7}{15} - \frac{9}{30} =$ ______

10. 2.875 + 0.789

11. 79.32 − 42.98

12. 14)493

Name ______________________________

# Tree Diagrams

Find the number of possible outcomes by making a tree diagram.

1. Higgins the clown has 3 hats (red, yellow, or blue) to choose from to match his 6 suits (gold, orange, blue, green, purple, and yellow). How many choices does he have?

   ______________________

2. Kathy has 6 different sweaters to wear with her 4 pairs of slacks. How many possible choices does she have?

   ______________________

3. Julia has a choice of using iceberg lettuce or red leaf lettuce for her birthday dinner. In addition, she can choose Italian, Russian, or French salad dressing. How many different outcomes are possible?

   ______________________

4. Thomas had 8 different choices of hats and coats. How many hats does he have? How many coats does he have?

   ______________________

   ______________________

   ______________________

For 5–6, you are choosing one of each.

5. Footwear choices:
   Shoes: navy, black, or brown
   Socks: white, black, or tan

   ______________________

6. Event choices:
   Events: sports, play, or movie
   Day: Saturday or Sunday

   ______________________

## Mixed Review

7. $(2 \times 4) + (2 \times 2) = ■$

   ______________________

8. Round 278,150 to the nearest thousand.

   ______________________

9. Compare. Write $<$, $>$, or $=$.

   379,560 ● 379,561

   ______________________

10. Solve for $n$.

    $20 - (12 - 2) = n$

    ______________________

Name ______________________



# Problem Solving Strategy

## Make an Organized List

Make an organized list to solve.

1. A spinner is labeled 6, 7, and 8. List all of the possible outcomes of spinning the pointer on the spinner 2 times.

______________________

______________________

2. Jeanne is writing a report on the computer. She has a choice of 5 different designs for the cover, and 3 different fonts for the report. How many possible ways of writing this report are there?

______________________

For 3–6, find the possible outcomes of spinning both pointers one time.

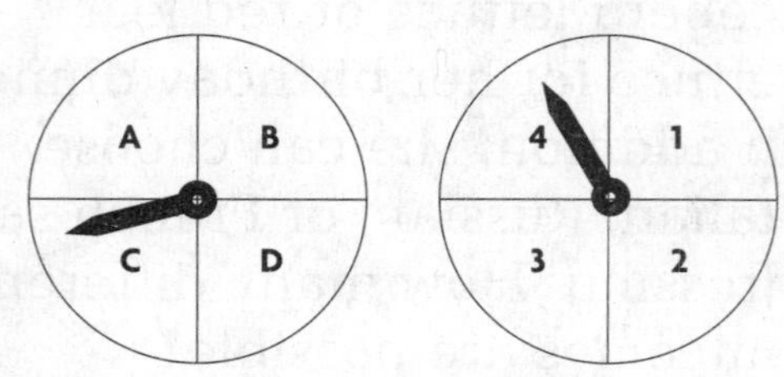


3. How many possible outcomes are there?

______________________

4. List all of the possible outcomes.

______________________

______________________

5. How many possible outcomes would there be if the spinners had 6 numbers?

______________________

6. How many of the possible outcomes include the letter F?

______________________

## Mixed Review

7. The race started at 6:53 P.M. and ended at 7:14 P.M. How long did the race take?

______________________

8. Find the sum of $15,666.22 and $14,323.56.

______________________

9. $(6 \times 4) - (3 \times 2) = \blacksquare$

______________________

10. Round 4,278,555 to the nearest ten thousand.

______________________

Name ______________________________



# More About Probability

## Use Data

For 1–4, use the spinner and the table.

| SPINNER EXPERIMENT—100 SPINS | | | | |
|---|---|---|---|---|
| **Outcome** | W | X | Y | Z |
| **Tally** | 卌 卌<br>卌 卌<br>// | 卌 卌<br>卌 卌<br>卌 // | 卌 卌<br>卌 卌<br>/ | 卌 卌<br>卌 卌<br>卌 卌 |

1. What is the mathematical probability of the pointer stopping on each letter on the spinner?

   *W* ______ *Y* ______

   *X* ______ *Z* ______

2. Use the data in the table. Find the probability of the pointer stopping on each letter in the experiment.

   *W* ______ *Y* ______

   *X* ______ *Z* ______

3. Use the table to find the probability of the pointer stopping on *W* in the experiment. How does this compare to the mathematical probability?

   ______________________________

4. Compare the probability in the experiment with the mathematical probability of the pointer stopping on *X*, *Y*, and *Z*.

   ______________________________

   ______________________________

   ______________________________

## Mixed Review

5. James is buying a new computer. He is choosing among 3 different hard drives, 4 different printers, and 5 modems. How many possible computer packages could he make?

   ______________________________

6. What kind of triangle is shown below?

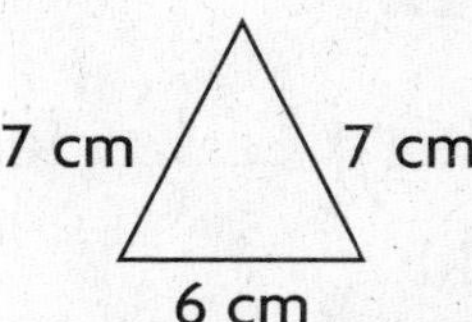


   ______________________________

Name ______________________________ 

# Test for Fairness

## Vocabulary

Complete the blank.

1. ________________ in a game means that one player is as likely to win as another. Each player has an equal chance of winning.

---

Look at the spinner. Each of the four players in a game chooses a number from 1, 2, 3, or 4 and scores 1 point when the pointer stops on his or her choice. Write *yes* or *no* to tell if each game is fair. Explain.

2. 

______________________________

______________________________

3. 

______________________________

______________________________

In Victor's game, players choose either 2 or 3. Players take turns tossing a number cube labeled 1–6. If a player chose 2 and rolls a 2, 4, or 6, he or she scores a point. If a player chose 3 and rolls a 3 or a 6, he or she scores a point.

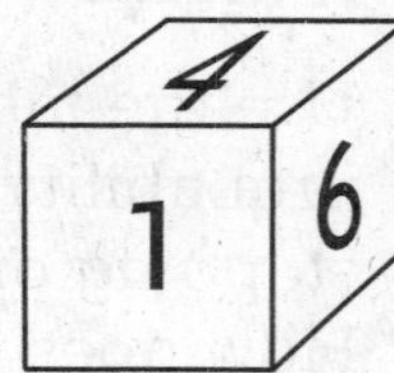


4. What is the probability of the player who chose 2 scoring a point? the player who chose 3?

______________________________

5. Why is this game not fair?

______________________________

______________________________

6. How could you change the game to make it fair?

______________________________

## Mixed Review

7. 156 inches = __?__ feet

8. 156 yards = __?__ feet

9. $\begin{array}{r} 951{,}511 \\ +\ 314{,}288 \\ \hline \end{array}$

10. $\begin{array}{r} 65{,}849 \\ \times\ \ 8 \\ \hline \end{array}$

11. $2\frac{1}{4} + 4\frac{5}{6} =$ ______

## Problem Solving Skill: Draw Conclusions

1. Jack and Kylie are playing a game with a bag of 10 marbles that are either yellow, green, black, or red. Jack earns 1 point when he pulls a yellow marble; Kylie earns 1 point when she pulls a green marble. Use the clues to find how many of each color of marbles are in the bag. Tell whether the game is fair. Explain.

**BAG OF MARBLES CLUES**

- The probability of drawing a red marble is $\frac{3}{10}$.
- The probability of drawing Jack's color is $\frac{2}{10}$.
- The probability of not drawing Kylie's color is $\frac{9}{10}$.

_______________________________________________

_______________________________________________

_______________________________________________

For 2–3, use the spinner.

Tom and Harry made up rules for a 2-player game using the spinner. Tell if the game is fair or not fair by using probability.

2. Tom's game:
Player 1 scores 1 point for an odd number.

Player 2 scores 1 point for a prime number.

_______________________________________________

_______________________________________________

_______________________________________________

_______________________________________________

3. Harry's game:
Player 1 scores 3 points for a composite number.

Player 2 scores 3 points for a factor of 6.

_______________________________________________

_______________________________________________

_______________________________________________

_______________________________________________

### Mixed Review

4. What are the factors of 21?

_______________________________________________

5. Rename $\frac{9}{2}$ as a mixed number.

_______________________________________________

6. Write 0.9 as a fraction.

_______________________________________________

7. List 5 multiples of 9.

_______________________________________________

Name ____________________



# Temperature: Fahrenheit

Use the thermometer to find the temperature in °F.

1. 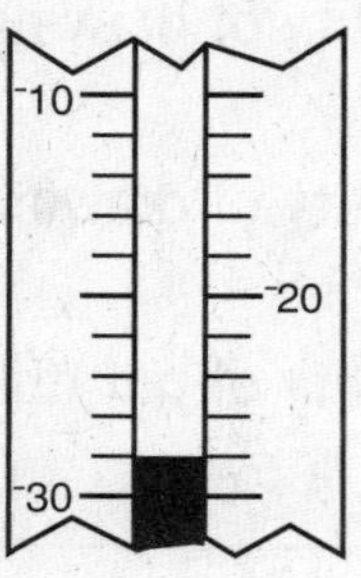


2. 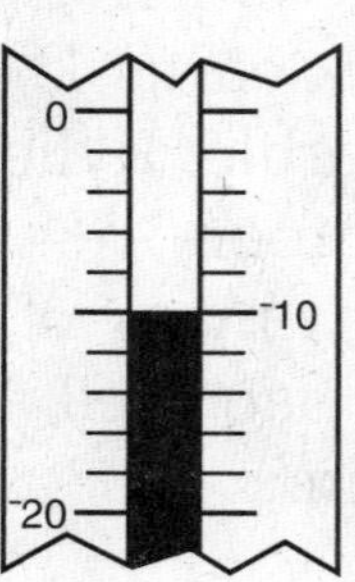


3. 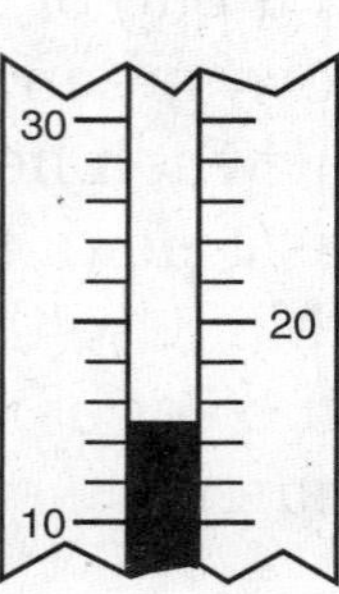


For 4–7, use a thermometer to find the change in temperature.

4. 0°F and 35°F

5. ⁻10°F and 10°F

6. ⁻5°F and 25°F

7. ⁻15°F and 30°F

Circle the temperature that is a better estimate.

8. A pot of boiling water
10°F or 212°F

9. A summer day in Florida
30°F or 95°F

10. An air-conditioned office building
75°F or 150°F

## Mixed Review

Find the value of *n*.

11. $n \div 30 = 20$

12. $(25 + 5) - (10 \div 2) = n$

13. $n \times 6 = 72$

14. $88 \div n = 8$

15. $37.4 + 12.9$

16. $72.8 + 15.2$

17. $27.4 - 18.6$

18. $29.9 - 11.9$

# Temperature: Celsius

Use the thermometer to find the temperature in °C.

1. 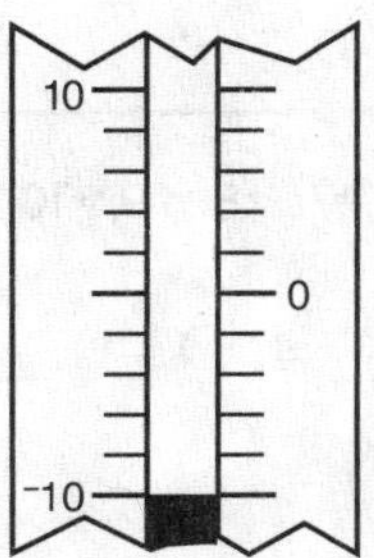


2. 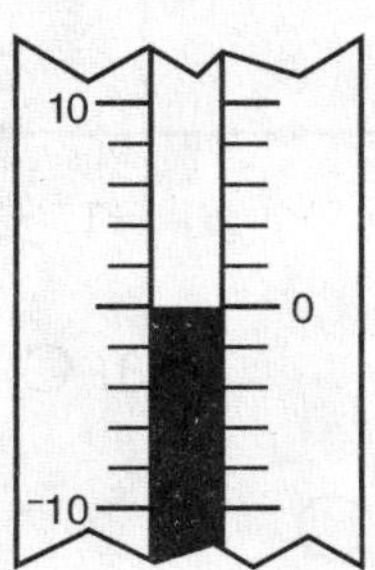


3. 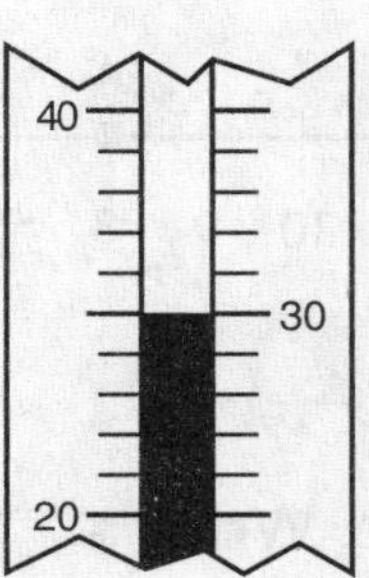


______ ______ ______

For 4–7, use a thermometer to find the change in temperature.

4. 67°C and ⁻55°C ______

5. 48°C and ⁻10°C ______

6. ⁻1°C and 50°C ______

7. ⁻15°C and 22°C ______

Circle the temperature that is a better estimate.

8. the ice at the ice rink

   ⁻1°C or 65°C

9. hot water in the tea kettle

   30°C or 100°C

10. a nice day for a picnic

   15°C or 80°C

**Mixed Review**

11. What is the change in temperature, in °F, from the boiling point (212°F) to the freezing point (32°F) of water? ______

12. How are these odd numbers alike? 5, 11, 17, 19, 23 ______

13. $25\overline{)17{,}650}$

14. $22\overline{)12{,}056}$

15. $17\overline{)4{,}952}$

16. $29\overline{)511{,}607}$

Name ______________________________

# Negative Numbers

Use the number line to name the number each letter represents.

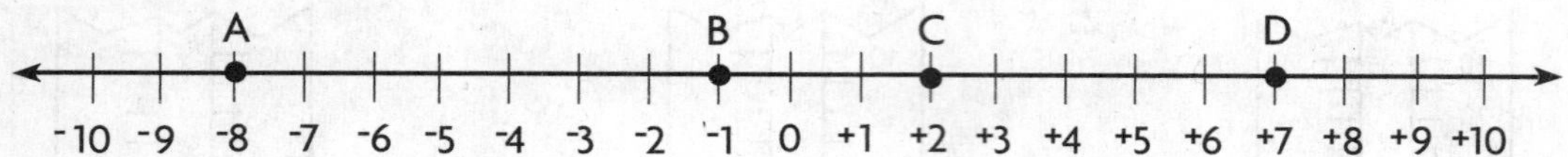


**1.** A = ______ **2.** B = ______ **3.** C = ______ **4.** D = ______

Compare. Write <, >, or = in each ○.

**5.** $^{-}8$ ○ $^{+}2$ **6.** $^{+}8$ ○ $^{+}2$ **7.** 0 ○ $^{+}2$ **8.** 2 ○ $^{+}2$

**9.** $^{+}9$ ○ $^{+}2$ **10.** $^{+}1$ ○ $^{+}8$ **11.** 0 ○ $^{-}1$ **12.** $^{-}2$ ○ $^{+}10$

Order the numbers from *least* to *greatest*.

**13.** 0, $^{-}2$, $^{-}10$, $^{-}5$

______________________

**14.** 0, $^{-}2$, $^{+}10$, $^{+}5$

______________________

**15.** $^{-}2$, $^{-}8$, $^{-}10$, $^{-}7$

______________________

**16.** $^{-}1$, $^{+}2$, $^{+}3$, $^{+}6$

______________________

Order the numbers from *greatest* to *least*.

**17.** $^{-}3$, 4, $^{-}5$, 3

______________________

**18.** 9, $^{-}7$, 2, $^{-}3$

______________________

## Mixed Review

**19.** List the factors of 18.

______________________

**20.** 36 × 100

______________________

**21.** What is the change in temperature from $^{-}8$°F to 8°F?

______________________

**22.** Which of these are composite numbers? 25, 31, 54, 79

______________________

Name ____________________



# Use an Equation

Do the values given make $y = 2x + 18$ true?
Write *yes* or *no*.

1. (1,20) ______ 2. (2,22) ______ 3. (3,24) ______ 4. (7,24) ______

5. (6,28) ______ 6. (4,26) ______ 7. (9,36) ______ 8. (11,30) ______

9. (5,28) ______ 10. (3,22) ______ 11. (8,32) ______ 12. (10,38) ______

Use the equation to complete each function table.

13. $y = 4x + 2$

| Input | *x* | 2 | 4 | 6 |
|---|---|---|---|---|
| Output | *y* | | | |

14. $y = (x + 1) - 1$

| Input | *x* | 1 | 2 | 3 |
|---|---|---|---|---|
| Output | *y* | | | |

15. $y = 2x + 5$

| Input | *x* | 3 | 6 | 9 |
|---|---|---|---|---|
| Output | *y* | | | |

16. $y = 3x + 22$

| Input | *x* | 1 | 2 | 3 |
|---|---|---|---|---|
| Output | *y* | | | |

17. $y = 9x + 1$

| Input | *x* | 1 | 4 | 7 |
|---|---|---|---|---|
| Output | *y* | | | |

18. $y = (x + 2) + 2$

| Input | *x* | 0 | 6 | 12 |
|---|---|---|---|---|
| Output | *y* | | | |

19. $y = (x - 1) + 2$

| Input | *x* | 1 | 5 | 9 |
|---|---|---|---|---|
| Output | *y* | | | |

20. $y = 3x + 14$

| Input | *x* | 2 | 4 | 6 |
|---|---|---|---|---|
| Output | *y* | | | |

21. $y = 8x + 6$

| Input | *x* | 1 | 2 | 3 |
|---|---|---|---|---|
| Output | *y* | | | |

## Mixed Review

Add.

22. 345 + 456

23. 3,657 + 1,737

24. 7,324 + 1,587

25. 3,542 + 8,732

26. 21,347 + 3,547

27. 13,216 + 543

28. 5,542 + 5,842

29. 3,211 + 6,544

30. 7,437 + 8,472

31. 9,813 + 7,134

Name ______________________________ 

# Graph an Equation

For 1–3, use the equation $y = x + 4$.

1. Complete this function table.

| Input | $x$ | 1 | 2 | 3 | 4 | 5 | 6 | 7 | 8 | 9 | 10 |
|---|---|---|---|---|---|---|---|---|---|---|---|
| Output | $y$ | | | | | | | | | | |

2. Write the input/output values as ordered pairs (x, y).

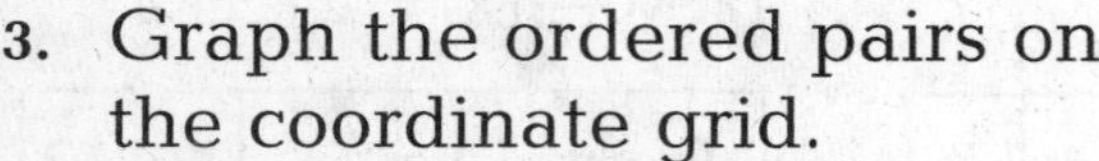

3. Graph the ordered pairs on the coordinate grid.

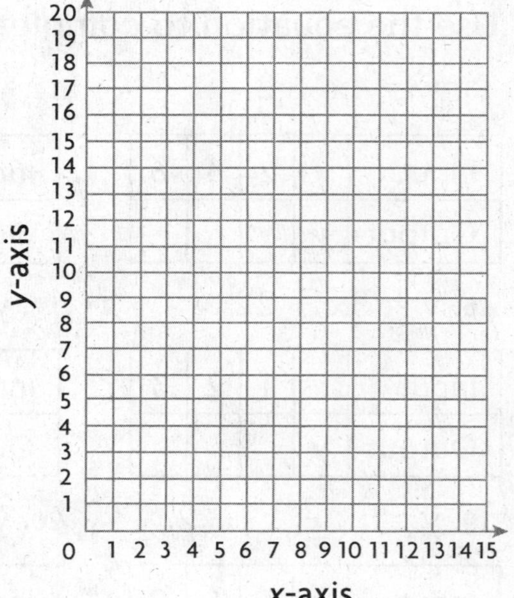


Make a function table. Write the input/output values as ordered pairs using the values 1 through 10 for $x$. Then graph the ordered pairs on the coordinate grid above.

4. $y = 2x$

| Input | $x$ | 1 | 2 | 3 | 4 | 5 | 6 | 7 | 8 | 9 | 10 |
|---|---|---|---|---|---|---|---|---|---|---|---|
| Output | $y$ | | | | | | | | | | |

**Mixed Review**

Solve.

5. $9\overline{)3{,}663}$  6. $25\overline{)10{,}150}$  7. $76\overline{)6{,}764}$

Name ____________________



# Problem Solving Skill

## Identify Relationships

For 1–3, use the function tables.

1. Describe the relationship between x and y.

____________________

____________________

| Input | $x$ | 1 | 2 | 3 | 4 | 5 |
|---|---|---|---|---|---|---|
| Output | $y$ | 2 | 4 | 6 | 8 | 10 |

2. Describe the relationship between x and y.

____________________

____________________

| Input | $x$ | 1 | 2 | 3 | 4 | 5 |
|---|---|---|---|---|---|---|
| Output | $y$ | 2 | 3 | 4 | 5 | 6 |

3. Describe the relationship between x and y.

____________________

____________________

| Input | $x$ | 1 | 2 | 3 | 4 | 5 |
|---|---|---|---|---|---|---|
| Output | $y$ | 4 | 8 | 12 | 16 | 20 |

For 4–5, use the graph at the right.

4. What is the relationship between the x and y values?

____________________

____________________

5. What is the value of y for x = 16?

____________________

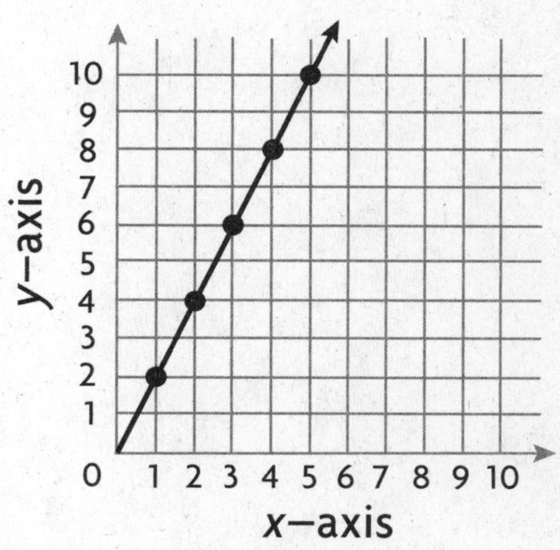




## Mixed Review

Order from *least* to *greatest*.

6. $\frac{1}{2}, \frac{2}{3}, \frac{1}{6}$ ____________

7. $\frac{3}{8}, \frac{3}{4}, \frac{3}{10}$ ____________

8. $\frac{7}{9}, \frac{2}{3}, \frac{6}{6}$ ____________